Cryptomimesis
The Gothic and Jacques Derrida's Ghost Writing

CW01080345

In the last thirty years the living-dead, the revenant, the phantom, and the crypt have appeared with increasing frequency in Jacques Derrida's writings and, for the most part, have gone unaddressed. In *Cryptomimesis* Jodey Castricano examines the intersection between Derrida's writing and the Gothic to theorize what she calls Derrida's "poetics of the crypt."

She develops the theory of cryptomimesis, a term devised to accommodate the convergence of philosophy, psychoanalysis, and certain "Gothic" stylistic, formal, and thematic patterns and motifs in Derrida's work that give rise to questions regarding writing, reading, and interpretation. Using Edgar Allan Poe's Madeline and Roderick Usher, Bram Stoker's Dracula, and Stephen King's Louis Creed, she illuminates Derrida's concerns with inheritance, revenance, and haunting and reflects on deconstruction as ghost writing.

Castricano demonstrates that Derrida's *Specters of Marx* owes much to the Gothic insistence on the power of haunting and explores how deconstruction can be thought of as the ghost or deferred promise of Marxism. She traces the movement of the "phantom" throughout Derrida's other texts, arguing that such writing provides us with an uneasy model of subjectivity because it suggests that "to be" is to be *haunted*. Castricano claims that cryptomimesis is the model, method, and theory behind Derrida's insistence that to learn to live we must learn how to talk "with" ghosts.

JODEY CASTRICANO is assistant professor in the Department of English at Wilfrid Laurier University.

Cryptomimesis

The Gothic and Jacques Derrida's Ghost Writing

JODEY CASTRICANO

McGill-Queen's University Press
Montreal & Kingston · London · Ithaca

ISBN 0-7735-2264-6 (cloth)
ISBN 0-7735-2279-4 (paper)

Legal deposit fourth quarter 2001
Bibliothèque nationale du Québec

Printed in Canada on acid-free paper

This book has been published with the help of a grant
from the Humanities and Social Sciences Federation
of Canada, using funds provided by the Social
Sciences and Humanities Research Council
of Canada.

McGill-Queen's University Press acknowledges
the financial support of the Government of Canada
through the Book Publishing Industry Development
Program (BPIDP) for its activities. It also
acknowledges the support of the Canada Council
for the Arts for its publishing program.

**National Library of Canada Cataloguing
in Publication Data**

Castricano, Carla Jodey
   Cryptomimesis: the gothic and Jacques Derrida's
   ghost writing
   Includes bibliographical references and index.
   ISBN 0-7735-2264-6 (bound) –
   ISBN 0-7735-2279-4 (pbk.)
   1. Derrida, Jacques. 2. Deconstruction. 3. Gothic
   revival (Literature). I. Title.
   B2430.S484C38 2001   194   C2001-901014-1

Typeset in Sabon 10.5/13
by Caractéra inc., Quebec City

Yesterday, you may remember, we made each other
a promise. I now recall it, but you already sense all
the trouble we will have in ordering all these presents:
these past presents which consist of the present of a promise,
whose opening toward the present to come is not that of
an expectation or an anticipation but that of commitment.

Jacques Derrida "The Art of Memoires" (47)

Contents

Acknowledgments

While I might trace this work back in spirit to a younger self who was fascinated with ghosts, secrets, underground chambers, trap doors, secret passages, and encrypted messages, I can also partially attribute my current theoretical interest in phantoms and haunted spaces to the fact that, when I was nearly ten, my father built a family room in our basement that included a bookcase that, when a concealed latch was released, swung open like a door. One could then walk through the opening which led through a passageway behind a wall. By following this passageway, one could emerge like a phantom through another concealed door on the opposite side of the room. These days, I'm told this house is haunted.

This book traces the trajectories of such hauntings. Over the past few years, I have been fortunate to have had the time, the encouragement, and the financial support to explore what was originally a childhood fascination with all things Gothic and which became a critical analysis of the social and cultural dimensions of haunting where these can be seen to resonate in literary and cultural studies, in philosophy, and psychoanalysis. Research and preparation of this work was originally assisted by a Graduate Fellowship from The University of British Columbia which went towards early speculations, and by a Doctoral Fellowship from the Social Sciences and Humanities Research Council of Canada which provided the opportunity to make manifest those intimations. More recently,

Wilfrid Laurier University provided further support in the form of a Postdoctoral Fellowship which facilitated the honing of the work, and a Book Preparation Grant which enabled me to bring this project to completion.

Thanks, too, are due to *Gothic Studies* for their permission to reprint from "Cryptomimesis: The Gothic and Jacques Derrida's Ghost Writing," an article derived from the manuscript which appeared in the April 2000 special issue of the journal, edited by Steven Bruhm, arising out of the wonderful Fourth Biannual conference of the International Gothic Association entitled "Gothic Spirits – Gothic Flesh," which was held in Halifax in August 1999.

Thanks are also due to the institutions that granted permission to use their materials: Quotations from *Jonas and Ezekial*, words and music by Amy Ray, copyright © 1992 EMI VIRGIN SONGS, INC. and GODHAP MUSIC (All Rights Controlled and Administered by EMI VIRGIN SONGS, INC. All Right Reserved, International Copyright Secured, Used by Permission). Quotations from W.B. Yeats, "The Second Coming" reprinted with the permission of Scribner, a Division of Simon & Schuster, Inc., from *The Poems of W.B. Yeats: A New Edition*, edited by Richard J. Finneran. Copyright © 1924 by The Macmillan Publishing Company, copyright renewed © 1952 by Bertha Georgie Yeats. I also want to thank Stephen King for his permission to reprint from *Pet Sematary* and Marsha DeFilippo, Stephen King's Assistant, for her good humour, patience, and assistance.

I am grateful to those who read this manuscript in its various incarnations, and who made invaluable comments: J.C. Smith, for his boundless enthusiasm and generous conversation; Peter Quartermain for sharing his love of poetics and Michael Zeitlin for his ongoing support. Thanks as well to Eric Savoy and Anne Williams for their thorough and thoughtful reading of the manuscript and to Joan McGilvray of McGill-Queen's University Press for keeping things on track. Thanks are due especially to Lorraine Weir who encouraged the work from its inception, served as a guide, and who asked provocative questions in person and in the margins. I also want to thank Margaret Eady for her generous response to a question that, years ago, opened a door and Nelia Tierney who was not afraid of talking with ghosts. Finally, thanks to Jacqueline Larson, for her keen editorial eye, for sharing her insights, and for the love and encouragement she offered throughout all the stages of this work.

Cryptomimesis

Convocation

Whoever wants to dream must mix all things together.

Albrecht Dürer

"To begin (writing, living) we must have death," writes Hélène Cixous in "The School of the Dead" (*Three Steps on the Ladder of Writing* 5). If I say that we have begun, will you understand? Drawn to Cixous's text I find that the page, which opens like a door upon these words, is marked with a ticket stub for a performance of Mozart's *Requiem*. But I did not know then what I know now: what we must have to begin. Otherwise, I might have continued to gaze at Frida Kahlo's *Pensando en la Muerte*, and, not seeing her death, or perhaps mine in hers, forget. But death tells us there is no meaning outside memory. Hélène Cixous says, "I like the dead, they are the door keepers who while closing one side 'give' way to the other," (5) the other being the dead in us, in whose memory we live and by whose death – or at least by the possibility of whose death – the "within me" or "within us" becomes possible. This spacing is what the dead "give." In mourning, says Derrida: "we weep precisely over what happens to us when everything is entrusted to the sole memory that is 'in me' or 'in us'" ("Mnemosyne" 33) – this interiority made always already possible only by the impossibility of "truly" mourning the (possibility of the) death of the other. "One *must* always begin by remembering," says Derrida; "it is the law" (35). If I say that we have begun, will you (remember to) understand?

One *must* always begin by remembering. And the way not to forget, says Cixous, is to write. Perchance to dream. Says Cixous,

"Dreams remind us that there is a treasure locked away somewhere and writing is the means to try and approach the treasure" (88). Approach can be terrifying, but this is the place where the other begins: where death enters the picture. Why else would Derrida say, writing's case is *"grave"* ("Plato's Pharmacy" 130)? Sometimes, when we are reading, we dream that we are writing but, says Cixous, "clearly this isn't true. We are not having the dream, the dream has us" (98). Whenever "the dream has us," we are filled with longing and disquiet for we are in the real of our desire which always takes the form of a secret. As in a dream, a rebus-text always says "something that is never said, that will never be said by anyone else and which you *unknow*; you possess the unknown secret" (Cixous 85, emphasis mine). You possess the unknown secret and you have forgotten that you have unknown it, all along. As dreams are always about unknowing, remembering, and forgetting, so, too, is a rebus-text. Thus, in the spirit of dreaming, Cixous writes, "when choosing a text I am called: I obey the call of certain texts or I am rejected by others. The texts that call me have different voices. But they all have one voice in common, they all have, with their differences, a certain music I am attuned to, and that's the secret" (5).

When texts call to us, what do they say and in whose voice do they speak? What calls to us in secret always takes the form of (a) haunting, especially as it concerns the other "in us" living on – so to speak – as a spectral effect of the text.

The First Partition:
Without the Door

jonas and ezekial hear me now
steady now i feel your ghost about
i'm not ready for the dead to show its face
whose angel are you anyway?

Jonas and Ezekial, The Indigo Girls

"'We *have put her living in the tomb!* ... I ... tell you that I heard her first feeble movements in the hollow coffin. I heard them – many, many days ago ...! *I tell you that she now stands without the door!*'" (Poe, "The Fall of the House of Usher" 547). Nearly two hundred years ago, Edgar Allan Poe's obsessive and overwrought Roderick Usher uttered the words that still resonate in the genre that has since come to be known as the American Gothic. Like many Gothic narratives, "The Fall of the House of Usher" concerns itself with haunting and issues of unresolved mourning, while featuring a vengeful return from the tomb. The image of Madeline of Usher's return from the dead foreshadows the continuing obsession with that trope in contemporary mass culture. Although some critics continue to disavow the Gothic as being subliterary and appealing only to the puerile imagination – Fredric Jameson refers to the Gothic as "that boring and exhausted paradigm" (289)[1] – others, such as Anne Williams, claim that the genre not only remains very much alive but is especially vital in its evocation of the "undead," an ontologically ambiguous figure which has been the focus of so much critical attention[2] that another critic, Slavoj Žižek, felt compelled to call the return of the living dead "the fundamental fantasy of contemporary mass culture" (22).[3]

The proliferation of works in contemporary mass culture evoking that "fantasy" – including fiction by Stephen King (*Pet Sematary* and *Salem's Lot*), Peter Straub (*Ghost Story*), and Anne Rice (*Interview With a Vampire*), as well as films by George Romero (*Night of the Living Dead, Dawn of the Dead)* and Francis Ford Coppola (*Bram Stoker's Dracula*) – all bear witness to Žižek's claim. However, while current critical attention, specifically feminist, psychoanalytic and cultural criticism, has been aimed at the social, sexual, and ideological dimensions of the return of the living-dead, haunting, and mourning, that same critical focus has been limited to the novel, short story, and film.[4] This critical limitation continues despite the fact that many of the familiar Gothic tropes and topoi have appeared not only in works of psychoanalysis,[5] but also in the discourse which has taken up the conditions of truth within Western metaphysics, namely Derridean deconstruction. It is curious that in the last thirty years the living-dead, the revenant, the phantom, and the crypt – along with their effects of haunting and mourning – have been appearing with increasing frequency in the writings of Jacques Derrida; it is even more curious that this inclination has, for the most part, gone unaddressed.[6]

Although Derrida has drawn attention to the way that literary studies are dominated by philosophical assumptions, I have not presumed to read Derrida's works with the aim of providing philosophical commentary. Instead, I propose the exploration of a certain terrain – a crypt, in fact – with an ear tuned to hearing how, in Derrida's work, (the) crypt functions as both the model and method (theory) – the structural machine or formal principle of a poetics, let's say – behind Derrida's production of "(s)cryptograms." While the notion of the crypt in this case recalls the psycho-t(r)opography suggested by Nicolas Abraham and Maria Torok in their discussion of the fantasy of incorporation, the concept also consists of what Nicholas Rand refers to as the "deposition of the time-honored distinction between inside and outside" (in Abraham and Torok, *The Wolf Man's Magic Word* lxviii). Although the term "(s)cryptogram" lends itself to a consideration of textuality as a performative theoretical space, I propose the term *cryptomimesis* to describe a writing practice that, like certain Gothic conventions, generates its uncanny effects through the production of what Nicholas Rand might call a "contradictory 'topography of inside outside'" (*topique des fors*) (lxviii). Moreover, the term cryptomimesis draws attention to a writing predicated upon encryption: the play of revelation and concealment lodged within *parts* of individual words.

A short digression is necessary here, if only to recall Derrida's reticence to employ any sign as "a transcendental pass, a password to open all doors, decipher all texts and keep their chains under surveillance" ("Passe-Partout" 12). In short, we must be wary of designating any single word as a "master key" (12). To do so would be "to predestine one's reading," which is what Derrida says about "the fearful reader, the reader in a hurry to be determined, decided upon deciding" ("Envois" 4). Specifically, Derrida extends a caveat to the reader who requires a "readable" itinerary, who disavows unpredictability and who, in fearing indeterminacy or undecidability, refuses the "call" of the other. This has to do with the structure of a text, with responding to the text of the other in a performative way.

This "performativity," says Derrida "calls for ... responsibility on the part of the readers. A reader is not a consumer, a spectator, a visitor, not even a 'receiver'" ("This strange institution" 51). Although Derrida is mindful that the moment of "transcendence" is "irrepressible," he is careful to point out that "it can be complicated or folded" (45). This remark directs our attention to the challenges presented by cryptomimesis, a practice of writing that simultaneously encourages and resists transcendent reading and, because it involves the play of phantoms, compels an irreducible plurality. Thus, to dwell upon the word "crypt" is not to designate either the word or the thing as the master key that will unlock the "truth." Rather it is to use "crypt" as a "positive lever," ("Positions" 41) which is how Derrida describes a word or term that facilitates a deconstructive reading. In her preface to *Of Grammatology*, Gayatri Spivak refers to such a positive lever thus:

If in the process of deciphering a text in the traditional way we come across a word that seems to harbor an unresolvable contradiction, and by virtue of being *one* word is made sometimes to work in one way and sometimes in another and thus is made to point away from the absence of a unified meaning, we shall catch at that word. If a metaphor seems to suppress its implications, we shall catch at that metaphor. We shall follow its adventures through the text and see the text coming undone as a structure of concealment, revealing its self-transgression, its undecidability. (lxxv)

In the case of cryptomimesis, to catch upon the word "crypt" as the "positive lever" is also to crypt upon the word "catch" – the term that alerts us to the cunning questions, the surprises, the deceptions, and the unexpected difficulties encountered in attempting to follow the "adventures" of a word through a text that is "coming undone as a structure of concealment." It is in the sense of performance, or performativity, therefore, that I understand the workings of the crypt in Derrida's writing.

Keeping these "adventures" in mind, I would argue that because of a certain economy – what I said I would call cryptomimesis – Derrida's works bear traces of being "ghost-written." By drawing upon such figures as the crypt, the phantom, and the living-dead, cryptomimesis utilizes and foregrounds the dynamics of haunting and mourning to produce an autobiographical deconstructive writing through the trope of "live burial," a trope that Eve Kosofsky Sedgwick describes as "a structural name for the Gothic salience of 'within'" (5).[7] Similarly, I want to suggest that cryptomimesis functions in terms of textual mime to produce, in part, what Gregory Ulmer refers to as "paraliterature" ("The Object of Post-Criticism" 94) – which he sees as being "a hybrid of literature and criticism, art and science..." (94) – and also what I prefer to call either "cryptography" or "phantomime," since these terms draw attention to the uncanny dimensions of a writing practice that takes place as a ghost or crypt-*effect* of haunting and mourning.

Because this work is exploratory and not to be considered exhaustive, I wish to avoid totalizing and thematizing gestures. I'm trying to do this in what Clint Burnham, in his aesthetics of Marxist theory, calls "a fairly 'Brutalist' manner." Says Burnham, "the watchwords [of such an aesthetics] might be: vulgar, reductive, simplistic and absolutist" (xiv). Because I am reading Derrida's works where, arguably, they intersect or "fold" into the Gothic in North American popular culture – taking as a premise that each is already inhabited, even haunted by the other, folded within the other – I have assumed, by a sleight of hand, that the works of popular culture, themselves generally considered "vulgar, reductive, simplistic and absolutist," have something to say about *Derrida's* writing. I have in mind Mark Wigley's claim that "the fissures that divide any text are actually folds that bind them to that which appears to be outside them, and it is precisely these folds that constitute the texts as such, producing the very sense of an inside and an outside that they subvert" (5).

And because I would argue that Derrida's "poetics of the crypt" exists in a certain relation of correspondence with the Gothic, the word *speculation* – and all it implies – should serve as a watchword directing our attention to what binds the two. The word *speculate* suggests that it is my task "to pursue an inquiry; to form a theory," but the word also draws our attention to the working of a certain economy which, on the one hand has always powered the Gothic engine and, on the other, has driven Derrida's concern with inheritance and legacy. Indeed, to speculate – derived from the Latin *specula*, a watch tower and *specere*, to look – is to engage in a certain financial transaction, one that involves risk of loss. My speculations lead me to consider that in both the so-called Gothic and in Derrida's work, what is at stake is the performance of a ghostly inheritance and a debt. This multiple performance also extends to the critical reception afforded the two since reading is likewise indebted or drawn into the performance of a phantom-driven debt.

The nature of the debt can best be appreciated in light of the English word *revenant* and the French *revenance*. These words bring to mind the theme of one returned from the dead and all that this implies as well as how that theme is bound to a certain economy: they have affinities with *revenue* and with *revenir* – from the French to come back or to *amount* to and thus to the notion of (financial) "return(s)" (Bass, "Glossary" to *The Post Card* xxviii). What returns, however, is always linked to desire, which is what Derrida means when he says that the crypt is "the *vault* of desire" ("*Fors*" xvii). The (economic) function of a crypt, like a vault, is to keep, to *save*, to keep *safe* that which would return from it to act, often in our place. Thus, wherever the theme of the living-dead arises, whether it be in so-called Gothic texts or in Derrida's works, the topic of revenance and desire cannot be separated from that of "ghostly inheritance," whether in the sense of what is received by descent or succession or what returns in the form of a phantom to tax the living. Slavoj Žižek's remark that the dead return from the grave to act as "collectors of some unpaid symbolic debt" (23) likewise draws attention to the element of obligation intrinsic to revenance while alluding also to the uncanniness of its discharge. How do the dead recover a debt? How do the living acquit themselves? Derrida suggests what is at stake in this contract by posing the question, "how to speculate on the debt of another coming back to, amounting to [*a soi revenant*] oneself?" ("To speculate" 263).

As usual, Derrida's question implies another. It leads us to the cutting edge of cryptomimesis. How, unless one *speculates* in a certain way, *can* one see "oneself" as *amounting* to the debt of another? How is such a sum determined? What currency is used as the medium of exchange? What financing supports such an undertaking? How will the debt be settled? What interest is due? Who will pay it? A certain doubling is, after all, implied. Here, the word *speculate* returns, reminding us of its affinity with *specular* – a word which in its turn evokes Lacan's conception of the mirror stage. And Lacan's notion of the mirror stage as being "formative of the function of the I" (1) shares an uncanny link with the word "spectre." But if the word *specular* draws attention to the misrecognition, anticipation, and retroaction of Lacan's temporal dialectic – its specular determinants – *spectre* suggests an uncanniness to that dialectic by drawing attention to the *spectral* nature of the "I" in terms of ghostly inheritance and an unresolved debt or promise. In effect, the very idea of the first-person singular, with all its claims to agency and consciousness, is irrevocably undermined when that pronoun is shown to be plurally determined. What then does it mean to speculate? What phantoms come into play? Especially when one writes? Derrida suggests that "speculation always speculates on some specter, it speculates in the mirror of what it produces, on the spectacle that it gives itself and that it gives itself to see. It believes in what it believes it sees: in representations" (*Specters of Marx* 146).

In an essay entitled, "The Lost Object – Me," Nicolas Abraham and Maria Torok's accounting of the "phantom" gives us insight into the gaps produced in (psycho) analysis by that spectral structure, and also into the workings of the economy of cryptomimesis:

The "shadow of the [love] object" strays endlessly about the crypt, until it is finally reincarnated in the person of the subject. Far from displaying itself, this kind of identification is destined to remain concealed ... Clearly, an identifying empathy of this type could not say its name, let alone divulge its aim. Accordingly, it hides behind a mask ... The mechanism consists of exchanging one's own identity for a fantasmic identification with the "life" – beyond the grave – of [a lost] object of love. (141–2)

These remarks regarding the phantom in terms of "reincarnation" – literally "re-fleshing" – can be fruitfully examined through the economy of the crypt, giving us to understand the nature of cryptomimetic writing.

If to *reincarnate* is to "bring [the] soul of (a person) into another body after death," for the purpose of working through "karma," there is a parallel between reincarnation and the "fatedness" of the "identifying empathy" mentioned by Abraham and Torok. Thus, the phantom – be it understood as either the "shadow of the object" or the "buried speech" of another" – returns *itself* in "the person of the subject" or, for that matter, the text. Through a certain form of inheritance – whether reincarnation or karma, destiny, *moira* – the phantom takes place through both the "I" and the body, which is "clearly ... [why it] could not say its name, let alone divulge its aim." So the concept of reincarnation is meaningful to the economy of the crypt since it involves the manifestation, *in the flesh*, of a tacit "agreement" with the dead.

In the Gothic, as in psychoanalysis, "contracts" with the dead always take the form of a *concealed* promise to do or not do. Haunting always implies a debt. Whether it's the ghost of the king in *Hamlet* or the ghost of Alfonso in *The Castle of Otranto*, haunting has an economic basis in the sense that the return of the dead from the grave, as Slavoj Žižek suggests, "materializes a certain symbolic debt beyond physical expiration" (23). In the American Gothic, Nathaniel Hawthorne's *The House of the Seven Gables* also demonstrates the economics of haunting when each heir to the property inherits the great guilt of his ancestor: "To the thoughtful mind there will be no tinge of superstition in what we figuratively express, [says the narrator,] by affirming that the ghost of a dead progenitor – perhaps as a portion of his own punishment – is often doomed to become the Evil Genius of his family" (13).

As this passage demonstrates, haunting implies not only debt but also guilt. Hawthorne's novel explores both personal and national guilt predicated upon capitalism; it thus forms a bond with Stephen King's *Pet Sematary*, a novel that takes up the issue of personal debt in the context of the colonial appropriation of indigenous lands. What both novels demonstrate is the sense of inexorable destiny upon which the Gothic turns to take up the issue of haunting and return.[8] Although such a return does not always depend on literal death, but a return of that which is "buried," it remains a function of the phantom rising out of the unconscious of another. The work of psychoanalyst Daniel Gunn, who has explored the role which language and the "I" play in the development of subjectivity, desire, and a sense of the body, has relevance here. Although his discussion focuses on individuals within families, specifically the production of ambivalence, it also draws attention to how the "phantom" manifests itself transgenerationally, institutionally, and thus, textually:

One thing a reading of Kafka or of Shakespearean comedy ... should give is the confidence to contend that parental demands need not necessarily be so self-evidently just or free of the ambivalence with which the child is trying to cope as psychoanalysis has tended to imply. What if parental demands are not inherent and natural, but are rather the *recycling of a previous demand which has been inadequately dealt with?* (74, emphasis mine)

In Abraham and Torok's terms, the phantom "reincarnated in the person of the subject" would be an analogue of Gunn's notion of the "recycling of a previous demand which has been inadequately dealt with." What Gunn and Abraham and Torok make clear is that both "reincarnation" and "recycling" are the basis of an economy in which return or haunting comes into play, as Gunn suggests, through "the body, and the 'I' through which the body attempts to gain access to language and desire" (76). Gunn's citation of one of psychoanalyst Maud Mannoni's dialogues with a patient illustrates what is at stake in this phantom economy of desire. The dialogue, says Gunn, "leads directly into the troubled heartland of the pronoun":

"I've got a headache," said a single child of three. (He had been brought to me [Maud Mannoni] because it was impossible to keep him in infant school where he endlessly complained about his head, and seemed ill, passive and in pain. In addition, he was subject to insomnia, for which his doctor could find no organic cause). With me he went through the same soliloquy.
"Who is saying that?" I asked him.
"I've got a headache," he went on repeating in the same plaintive tone.
"Where? Show me where your head aches." It was not a question he'd ever been asked.
"There," he said, pointing to his thigh near the groin.
"And whose head's that?"
"It's Mummy's." (qtd. in Gunn 77)[9]

What we have is a kind of phantom limb that is not the result of amputation but of what rises up out of the unconscious of another. The "returns" within this economy are clearly uncanny. Yet though they are fundamental to psychoanalysis, returns like this are also crucial to the Gothic where haunting usually takes the contractual form of a ghostly inheritance. Such a ghostly inheritance is also fundamental to Derrida whose thoughts regarding the crypt's function suggest that cryptomimesis – like the crypt – is *itself*, "that *contract* with the dead" ("*Fors*" xxxviii, emphasis mine).

POETICS OF THE CRYPT

Of course, to some, the desire to juxtapose the name of Jacques Derrida with that of Stephen King, Peter Straub, George Romero, and even Count Dracula might seem monstrous in itself but then, as Donna Haraway suggests, "monsters have always defined the limits of community in Western imaginations" (180). There are many wings in the Gothic mansion. Without the door, the structure lies open to speculation. For better or for worse, I have taken on the task of drawing together an unlikely couple, namely Jacques Derrida and the phantoms of popular culture for purposes of theorizing what I have called Derrida's poetics of the crypt which lends itself to a consideration of both the dynamics of mourning and haunting that characterize Derrida's compositional mode as well as the way that the "crypt" (and all it implies), so integral to the Gothic genre, delineates the uncanny spatial topography of Derrida's work. If the familiar elements of Gothic fiction – dreams, crypts, phantoms – are present in Derrida's work, so much more so are the dynamic and uncanny structural principles of the Gothic: a sense of the unspeakable; a correspondence between dreams, language, and writing; and traces of the theme of live burial, all of which Eve Kosofsky Sedgwick describes as fundamentally Gothic (37–96).

Briefly, the works of Derrida to which I shall refer "call" to us with the story of their own plural, fluid, and simultaneous production. Encrypted and encrypting, these works lead us to reflect upon the nature of language and of writing in spatial terms (of the crypt) that, in turn, produce a radical psychological model of the individual and collective "self" configured in spectral terms of phantoms and haunting. In works such as "*Fors*," "Cartouches," *Memoires for Paul de Man*, *Glas*, *The Ear of the Other*, "Living

On," and *Specters of Marx*, spectral tropes and topoi demonstrate that the logic of haunting and the notion of the return of the living-dead are implied in "individual" being – the so-called subject – as well as in historical, social, and cultural realms. They suggest a certain intersection between the notion of the "subject" and (inter-) textuality in terms of spectral effects. Written from the border between incorporation and introjection, the texts that I will discuss[10] are cryptophoric: by setting free certain shadows, they participate in the staging of the enigma of a generation in the throes of unresolved mourning.

One final caveat. Of course, there are many "Derridas" and one must be careful of ascribing to Derrida (the one who signs) what, in effect, the cultural text "Derrida" accomplishes. I refer specifically to my reading of Derrida's work in English rather than in French. The "Derrida" to whom I am referring should, therefore, be understood as a textual effect of (an English) translation. As Mark Wigley says, "the very sense of something original is but an effect of translation, the translation actually producing what it appears to simply reproduce" (3). Although my intention is to theorize what I am calling Derrida's poetics of the crypt, I also have a supplementary goal to call attention to what makes such a project viable, namely the peculiar resonance which occurs between a meeting of two trajectories: "Derrida" *in America* and (American) Gothic literature.

Although Derrida warns against making the assumption that one knows what is meant or defined by the word "America," it is clear that he considers the place he provocatively calls "the new Europe" (*Specters* 40) to be an effect of the Enlightenment's dream. In this sense, America is the excess or beyond of a Europe that is yet to come. This is what Joseph Riddel means when he describes "'America' as ... not so much a history of what occurred as a dream to be arrived at. It is a point of arrival infinitely deferred by the act of searching for it" (99). In these terms, America was never discovered but was *invented*. The same holds true of American literature which Riddel contends is "a futural other, to which the actual literary texts we have and study are kinds of prefaces or notes toward; prologues written both after and before the fact, before the letter" (21). "American" or "America" become not only the name of a certain displacement that is integral to Derrida's thought but also an allegory of haunting. Riddel points this out, saying

There is a "scene" recalled in one of the autobiographical "Envois" of Jacques Derrida's *The Post Card* that might remind us of the displacement "literature" effects within contemporary discourse, and the performative role that Poe in particular, but also American literature in general, and even the place and name "America," are made to play in that discourse. It is a scene and story of place and displacement, an allegory, as it were, of history, discourse, criticism, and of a certain problematics of accounting – of reading and writing the dead. (17)[11]

It is evident that Derrida, like Riddel, perceives "America" in similar terms. In "Mnemosyne" (in *Memoires for Paul De Man*) for example, Derrida refers to the problem of defining "America" and calls the United States

that historical space which today, in all its dimensions and through all its power plays, reveals itself as being undeniably the most sensitive, receptive, or responsive space of all to the themes and effects of deconstruction ... In the war that rages over the subject of deconstruction, there is no front, there are no fronts. But if there were, they would all pass through the United States ... In this fiction of truth, "America" would be *the title of a new novel* on the history of deconstruction and the deconstruction of history. (18, emphasis mine)

With Derrida's remarks in mind, it seems appropriate that certain of his works be read as intersecting with the Gothic in "America" since it is this encounter that produces a sense of the uncanny correspondence which, to recall Riddel's phrase, is a scene "of reading and writing the dead." Both Riddel's and Derrida's remarks suggest that the United States can best be spoken of in terms of "literature," since "America," according to Riddel is "always already a text without origin, a translation of a translation" (100). Thus, if *America* were "the title of a new novel," that novel would be "in progress" because in this formulation, *America* would be "the beyond of modernism, a literature burdened with producing a past it never had, except in the figure of revolution, in order to mime that past into a future it lagged behind" (Riddel, 101). Similarly, if America is the dream of Europe, *America* is also a rebus-text, perhaps a Gothic "novel" based on the dream of "reading and writing the dead." I hope to draw attention to Derrida's affinity with the Gothic in America and to suggest ways of reading his work in terms of its participation in the staging of a cultural imaginary in which the trope of the living-dead and their return from the grave materializes a certain unpaid symbolic debt.

TRANSGENERATIONAL HAUNTING: LIVING ON

The phantom and the revenant are not merely worn-out conventions of the Gothic. Rather, these figures draw attention to an uncanny dimension implicit in Fredric Jameson's assertion that postmodern culture functions as "a world transformed into sheer images of itself" (18). These "images" also suggest what, on a collective and social level, is at stake in Slavoj Žižek's remark that "certain state or ideological apparatuses ... although they are clearly anachronistic ... persist because *they do not know* [*that they are dead*]" (44). Žižek and Jameson are describing a phenomenon with which the Gothic has always been concerned – what might best be called *transgenerational haunting*, that manifestation of the voices of one generation in the unconscious of another – but their assertions also suggest that the works of the Gothic in popular culture might lend themselves to an understanding of how certain of Derrida's works simultaneously stage, theorize, and thereby participate in another variation of transgenerational haunting.

In a certain sense, to be haunted is to be called upon. According to Walter Benjamin a text "calls" to us for translation. In this way, a text, Derrida would say, "lives on." It also means that when it is signed by the other, or "translated," a text *"comes back"* in a certain way – a phenomenon which always occurs, Derrida says, when "another makes use of [a text] or cites it" ("Roundtable on Translation" 158). But the text that comes back is never the same text; it is, thus, "never an echo ... that comes back ... or, if there is, it's always distorted" (158). It's always "distorted" because, being translated, it has signed itself in the *ear* of the other – a (textual) structure which is, according to Derrida, both "uncanny" and "double" ("Otobiographies" 33). Thus, when we are called by a certain text, it is perhaps, to recall Cixous, with an ear "attuned" to "a certain music" that the spectral *signature* comes in/to play (which might be a way of eventually describing *my* idiosyncratic engagement with "Jacques Derrida" in "America"). A spectral signature can therefore be thought of in terms of what Esther

Rashkin, in *Family Secrets and the Psychoanalysis of Narrative*, calls "transtextuality," a term she proposes for "the specific kind of intertextual relationship at work in narratives organized by phantoms" (45). What is so uncanny about this "relationship" is that it can be seen shimmering in the slippage suggested by the word "by" when it comes to thinking about the organization of such narratives. In other words, we are "called" by certain texts because they are organized *by* phantoms.

Whenever a text "calls" to us, it is for the purpose of (doing) dreamwork with ghosts, phantoms, spectres, revenants: all those whose return prompts us to remember that dreamwork is also memory work which manifests itself in terms of haunting. Although what haunts us is what we inherit, the legacy is always contradictory. Derrida suggests that it takes the form of a double bind: secrecy and choice. Thus, whenever a text calls to us, we are being asked to confirm an inheritance and to respond to an injunction. We begin by choosing. This "choice" is always double-edged for it takes the form of invitation and resistance. How are we to respond to the call of a text which is also a resistance? Our response is the basis of haunting. Nicholas Royle suggests the uncanniness of reading and interpretation when, in *Telepathy and Literature*, he writes, "What would it mean for a text to be a ghost? Or for a text to have prescience, foresight, foreknowledge" (12). In *Specters of Marx*, Derrida's remarks illuminate this double-bind:

An inheritance is never gathered together, it is never one with itself. Its presumed unity, if there is one, can consist only in the *injunction* to *reaffirm by choosing*. "One must" means *one must* filter, sift, criticize, one must sort out several different possibilities that inhabit the same injunction. And inhabit it in a contradictory fashion around a secret. If the readability of legacy were given, natural, transparent, univocal, if it did not call for and at the same time defy interpretation, we would never have anything to inherit from it. We would be affected by it as by a cause – natural or genetic. One always inherits from a secret–which says "read me, will you ever be able to do so?" (16)

The answer to this question is both yes and no. To be called by a text is to be drawn into the crossroads of secrecy and desire. This paradox is what Shoshana Felman has in mind when she asks "where does it resist? Where does a text ... precisely ... make no sense, that is, resist interpretation? Where does what I see and what I read resist my understanding? Where is the ignorance – the resistance to knowledge – located? And what can I learn from the locus of that ignorance?" (80).

In other words, the secret best kept is the one from ourselves. As for inheritance, Felman's remarks can draw attention to one aspect of haunting that *remains at work* even when it is unconscious or disavowed. Where Felman asks "what can I learn" from those texts that resist "understanding," Hélène Cixous might respond that these texts "teach us how to die" (*Three Steps* 22) because, in effect, they show that "each of us, individually and freely, must do the work that consists of rethinking what is your death and my death, which are inseparable" (12). To understand that "your death and my death" are "inseparable" is to perceive that what constitutes the division between "self" and "other" is death. In these terms, a text that "teach[es] us how to die" would also be a text from which we might learn to live. But learning, of course, is always already a question of haunting and inheritance.

In *Specters of Marx*, Derrida speaks of the spectral dynamics implicit in the call of texts that teach us how to die. More importantly, he asserts that any discussion of "ourselves" – including "you," "me" "us" and "I" – is spectrally determined, especially when it is unconscious or disavowed: "*To learn to live*: a strange watchword. Who would learn? From whom? To teach to live, but to whom? Will we ever know? Will we ever know how to live and first of all what 'to learn to live' means?" (xvii).

To begin (writing, living) we *must* have death. We must have death because it is "only from the other and by death" (xviii) says Derrida that we come into the configuration of "ourselves." To understand this, however, we must "learn to live *with* ghosts, in the upkeep, the conversation, the company, or the companionship" (xvii).

Derrida's insistence that we have "to learn to live *with* ghosts" does not mean merely a being-with but, as he suggests, "this being-with specters would also be, not only but also, a *politics* of memory, of inheritance, and of generations" (xix). Written to address today's disavowal of Marx, these reflections come out of Derrida's reading of Marx's "spectropoetics" – Marx's obsession with ghosts, spectres and spirits – in which Derrida, whose preoccupation with the return of the dead out-gothicizes the Gothic, argues that we are all heirs of Marx and that it is our responsibility to sift through our inheritance: the possible legacies that come to us in the spirit of Marxism(s). To learn to live *with* ghosts is to rethink ourselves through the dead or, rather, through the return of the dead (in us) and thus through haunting.

How, then, to recall Derrida, *are* we "to learn to live," especially when we consider the uncanny implications of Derrida's questions when asked from the perspective of mourning, inheritance, and haunting?

Derrida's questions remind us that we ignore the dead at our peril. To ask, *Who* would learn? and *From whom?* is to draw attention to phantom structures of subjectivity and to thereby launch an inquest into the undecidability of "identity." Who would learn, indeed, if the "I" with which one speaks is a "revenant" that is yet to come? By drawing our attention to how, as Esther Schor puts it, "the dead shape the lives we are able to live" (4) the question, "To teach to live, but *to whom?*" reminds us of a certain ghost story – one which can but feature a return from the dead as a debt, as a promise, and as a translation.

INHERITANCE, LEGACY, GHOSTS, HAUNTING

Derrida's work can be seen to take up what Anne Williams calls "that quintessentially Gothic issue – legitimate descent and rightful inheritance" (239). In fact, Derrida's concern with inheritance turns upon the (dissimulation of the) proper name as a site of "haunting" since, as Derrida remarks, "Only the name can inherit, and this is why the name, to be distinguished from the bearer, is always and a priori a dead man's name, a name of death" ("Otobiographies" 7). In Derrida's work, however, the "name of death" is not only multiple and "feminine," it is also *autobiographical*, giving us to think of "autobiography" as a spectral effect (of writing) that renders sexuality/gender undecidable. Thus, when Derrida writes, "everything I write is terribly autobiographical" ("Roundtable on Autobiography" 72), the emphasis on the "terribly" cannot be underestimated since, as he asserts,

the adverb must be given the meaning that comes directly from its nomi-native root – "in a manner that inspires terror" (one will have to wonder who or what inspires terror, and in whom) – rather than its more familiar, banalized meaning, as, for example, when one wants to signify the intensity of one's attachment to someone or something. Yet, notice that even the latter sense implies excess or extreme. (72)

The parenthetical remark – "one will have to wonder who or what inspires terror, and in whom" – makes the link between haunting and autobiography. This link is one reason why Derrida speculates that "one writes not only for those yet to live but for the dead.... I think one writes also *for* the dead" ("Roundtable on Autobiography" 53). Here, as elsewhere in Derrida's writing, the preposition stages an undecidability. Firstly, the word *for* draws attention to its role in *"Fors"* – Derrida's foreword to and an elaboration of Nicolas Abraham and Maria Torok's analysis of Freud's most well-known analysand in *The Wolf Man's Magic Word: A Cryptonymy* – in which Derrida plays upon the word *fors*. In the French expression *le for intérieur, for* designates the inner heart: subjective interiority. In the plural, *fors* – derived from Latin *foris* – is an archaic preposition meaning "except for, barring, save" ("Translator's Note to 'Fors'" xi). Thus, to write "for(s)" the dead is to anticipate our own. Similarly, the word "for" in English suggests that one writes not only as an agent for the dead, but also that the dead *write in our place*, a notion that is suggested by another of Derrida's assertions, *"departed* is the subject" ("Cartouches" 190). That is, in the case of the proper name, which is "not to be confused with the bearer," one writes *as* the (still living) dead, in their name or in their memory which is what Derrida implies when he says, "every name is the name of someone dead or, of a living someone whom it can do without" ("Roundtable on Autobiography" 53). Writing, therefore, necessarily draws attention to itself in terms of inheritance, legacy, and haunting.

The proper name is, however, not only multiple; it can, if it is the name of a phantom, also be secret or barred from consciousness. Staging the signature(s), then, becomes a complicated affair since it is no longer only a matter of spacing – wherein it is "the ear of the other that signs" (51) – but rather of inscribing or letting be inscribed (the unspeakable name of) an altogether Other – a phantom, shall we say, or a living-dead – (returning as inheritance) in place of the "subject." This structure is what Abraham and Torok refer to when they are speaking in terms of the phantom and the analysand: "It takes some time to understand [that the

analysand] speaks and lives someone else's words and affects"
("The Lost Object – Me" 150). Thus, when Derrida says, "everything I write is terribly autobiographical," we are left with the
question Derrida's pronoun suggests: *whose autobiography are we
talking about?*

One might argue that Derrida's concerns intersect or fold into
those of the Gothic at the point where each approaches the issue
of inheritance, legacy, and haunting precisely through the figure of
a ghost, phantom, or revenant who, having returned from the dead,
haunts the living with unspeakable secrets – unspeakable because
they are unconscious – which were taken to the grave but which
return via the agency of the proper name.[12] In the case of the Wolf
Man, as Gregory Ulmer points out, what is unspeakable is sealed
in a psychic vault as a "word thing" which then, says Ulmer,
"functions as the Wolf Man's name, naming the singularity of his
desire, dissociated entirely from the names of his fathers, both civil
and psychoanalytic" (*Applied Grammatology* 62). However, as
Ulmer points out, even "a word treated as a thing that is unspeakable ... achieves utterance by means of a complex translation
process" (62). "To achieve utterance by a complex translation
process" is to effect a certain return which, for Derrida, takes the
form of a phantom. In his reading and re-reading of Marx, Derrida
speculates at great length about the fact that the first noun that
appears in *The Manifesto of the Communist Party* is "specter"
(*Specters* 4). When Derrida finally noticed the word, he was
shocked to realize he had just "discovered, in truth ... just remem-
bered what must have been haunting [his] memory" (4). Where his
reading of Marx becomes a "complex translation process" it comes
in the form of a phantom: "I knew very well there was a ghost
waiting there" (4). In Derrida's work, the notion of the phantom
has Gothic affinities in that the return of the dead from the grave
and haunting can be understood to demonstrate, for better or for
worse, what is at stake when, to recall Ulmer above, "a word
treated as a thing that is unspeakable achieves utterance."

In Gothic fiction and film, what "achieves utterance" is also,
generally speaking, that which *horrifies*. It horrifies because it is
unspeakable and it haunts for the same reason. That which is
unspeakable can, according to Abraham and Torok in their discussion of the metapsychology of secrets, "determine the fate of an
entire family line," (*The Shell and the Kernel* 140). This is what is

at stake in Derrida's reading of Marx in terms of ghosts, haunting, and inheritance. According to Derrida, Marx's work might be thought of as a virtual space of spectrality which stages "a certain dramaturgy of modern Europe" (5) in terms of haunting. It is "the experience of the specter, [says Derrida,] that is how Marx, along with Engels, will have ... thought, described or diagnosed" this performative comprising the "great unifying projects" of modern Europe (4–5). To have recourse to a certain spirit of Marxism, says Derrida is also to "engender new ghosts" (87) since "one *must assume the inheritance* of Marxism, assume its most 'living' part, which is to say, paradoxically, that which continues to put back on the drawing board the question of life, spirit, or the spectral, of life-death beyond the opposition between life and death" (54). To put the question of life, spirit, and the spectral back on the "drawing board" is to draw attention to the line which is drawn "between life and death" in terms of the signature. As Gregory Ulmer points out in *Of Grammatology*, "it is never possible to decide who or what signs" (132). Since the signature of the proper name can also conceal another signature, we might call these moments of indecision "ghost writing" because they call attention to what is at stake when Ruth Parkin-Gounelas claims that "Derrida's text is haunted by Marx, just as Marx's texts ... are haunted by Max Stirner, whose own texts, Derrida tells us, are haunted by Hegel's" (127–43). To see how Derrida signs Marx, we must first consider what it means to write with ghosts.

TO WRITE WITH GHOSTS

It would be appropriate at this time to recall Derrida's contention that "it is necessary to introduce haunting into the very construction of a concept" (*Specters* 161). On the one hand, the word *haunting* is, as Mark Wigley points out, "etymologically bound to that of 'house'" (163). On the other hand, the comment suggests that haunting is to concept as haunting is to house. That is, the notion of haunting involves the "construction" or creation of an *inside*. This is what Mark Wigley implies when he claims that haunting is "always the haunting of a house," or of a "space" since, he continues, "space is understood as that which houses" (163). Haunting, then, implies interiority: the necessary construction of an "inside" whether of a house, a text, a thesis, a system of representation, or a "subject." This is what Derrida suggests when he says, "haunting [marks] the very existence of Europe. It would open the space and the relation to self of what is called by this name, at least since the Middle Ages" (*Specters* 4). But by what mechanism does an "inside" come about? To the extent that thought, or memory – that we, *ourselves* – are ineluctable measures of a spacing, we are drawn into a consideration of haunting that *necessarily* includes mourning since, according to Derrida, "only through [the] experience of the other, and of the other as other who can die, leaving in me or in us this memory of the other," does the "me" or the "us" arise ("Mnemosyne" 33).

Haunting and all it implies is a trope that is integral to the Gothic genre, but it also functions to link writing with a return from the dead. Where Derrida thinks in terms of haunting, he does so through Nicolas Abraham and Maria Torok's theory of the "phantom," and the crypt, both of which are psychic structures of incorporation. When Abraham and Torok speak of the fantasy of incorporation, they draw upon the notion that *words* of desire can act as phantoms when they are excluded from the preconscious. This is also what Derrida implies when he says, "as for language, it inhabits the crypt in the form of 'words buried alive'" ("*Fors*" xxxv) – a remark that makes Derrida sound every bit as "Gothic" as, for example, Edgar Allan Poe whose works consistently evoke similar concerns.[13] As far as psychoanalysis is concerned, however, Derrida is referring to how excluded words "migrate" to the unconscious where, as Abraham and Torok would argue, they work as if they were representations of repressed *things*. It is their *absence* in the preconscious which signifies that the trauma never took place.[14] Incorporation occurs when the process of introjection is blocked by conflicting desires. The inaccessible object of desire is then incorporated as a "fantasy" within the body and hidden from the ego in a "crypt" from which it returns to haunt either through other words-that-hide or through somatic symptoms that can be read, as Freud pointed out, as the literalization of a figure of speech.

In Freud's terms the return of the repressed relies on the concept of latency – that is, behind an expressed emotion lies one which is contrary and thus, repressed. What has been repressed will eventually force its way back into consciousness. According to Abraham and Torok, however, the concepts of the crypt and the phantom give us to understand that, as Nicholas Rand points out, "actual events are treated as if they had never occurred. Instead of the shifting fortunes of opponents locked in combat ... [as in the Freudian structure of oppositions], what matters is the preservation of a shut-up or excluded reality. This is why [Abraham and Torok] speak of *preservative* repression, or the topography of encrypted secrets, and contrast it with Freud's concept of *dynamic* repression" (*The Shell and the Kernel* 18). In these terms, the return of the deeply repressed consists of a return of a "phantom," an entity which might as well be that of an Other. In this context, consider the uncanniness of Abraham and Torok's "reading" of the Wolf Man in *The Wolf Man's Magic Word*:

The person in despair who, rendered helpless by depression, consulted Freud in 1910 was not quite the same as the one who lay on his couch a few days later. They appeared to be two separate people in one, without either of them representing the basic identity of the Wolf Man. Although often having the same desires as he, they remained nevertheless distinct from him. As a result, a paradox emerged in which the sexual license loudly claimed by one would only reinforce repression in the other. We suspected the existence of a cohabitation, at the core of the same person, involving his elder sister's [as well as his father's] image and his own. Two people in a third one. (3)

Two people in a third one: an uneasy model of subjectivity, to be sure. "What returns to haunt is," as Esther Rashkin points out in her discussion of Abraham and Torok's theory of the phantom, "the 'unsaid' and the 'unsayable' of *an other*. The silence, gap, or secret in the speech of someone else [is what becomes the phantom who, thus,] 'speaks' in the manner of a ventriloquist ... (28)." This notion of ventriloquism is intriguing to keep in mind when considering Derrida's writing practice, especially where it is described in terms of inscribing or letting be inscribed the altogether other – a feminine interlocutor – by displacing a certain masculinity that situates itself *before* the differentiation of masculine and feminine.[15] This is why Derrida remarks that "each time it is she, it is you who signs the text by receiving it" ("Roundtable on Autobiography" 79). Writing the altogether other, in Derrida's case, is predicated upon a re-thinking of the subject as a "non-place," a thought that runs contrary to the traditional notion that the subject takes place (Wigley 176).

While Abraham and Torok's theory of the phantom calls into question Freud's notion of the universality of psychic development, it also leaves the door ajar on the question of the so-called subject – a question which Derrida constantly poses – who is assumed to be fully conscious and, hence, fully self-knowable. If the subject is a non-place or a haunted site, analysis becomes an uncanny affair. As Esther Rashkin points out:

Effecting transference in the presence of a phantom is all the more challenging since the playing out or actualization of the internal drama must occur not between the analyst and the patient ... but between the analyst and the patient's ancestor (or whoever else may have originated [a] secret). At stake for the analyst is assuring that the individual "on the couch," metapsychologically speaking, is the one responsible for the formation of the phantom. Outlandish as this may seem, this often means analyzing, via the mediating presence of the patient, someone who is long since deceased. (*Family Secrets and the Psychoanalysis of Narrative* 32–3)

This configuration, in which the unspeakable is silently transmitted to someone else, is appropriately called the phantom. According to Torok, the phantom calls into question the notion of the integrity of the "I," since it "is alien to the subject who harbours it" ("Story of Fear" 181). The so-called subject, therefore, is haunted by the "living-dead knowledge of *someone else's secret*" (Abraham "The Intermission of 'Truth'" 188). This is an especially interesting remark when it is coupled with Stephen King's assertion that all horror stories deal with "secrets best left untold and things best left unsaid" and yet, he continues, they "all promise to tell us the secret" (*Danse Macabre* 50). Because a Gothic story is tacitly constituted by the idea that the phantom might be "someone who is long since deceased," Anne Williams, in *Art of Darkness: A Poetics of Gothic*, argues that the collected works of Freud are profoundly Gothic in their concerns with the family romance.

One might make a similar argument regarding the works of Nicolas Abraham who, for example, says, "to be sure, all the departed may return, but some are destined to haunt" ("Notes on the Phantom" 171). The argument certainly extends to Jacques Derrida, whose texts often recall the uncanny aspects of certain Gothic tropes. In "Cartouches," Derrida's remarks call up the image of Dracula, the paradigmatic figure of the living-dead in popular culture: "what can one desire of a coffin if not to have it for one's own, to steal it, to put oneself inside and see oneself in it?" (191). Earlier I said that according to Walter Benjamin, a text calls to us for a translation. If this is the case, how am I to explain what it is that "calls" to me when I "hear" Jacques Derrida say, "the inhabitant of a crypt is always a living dead, a dead entity we are perfectly willing to keep alive, but *as* dead, one we are willing to keep, as long as we keep it, within us, intact in any way save as living" (*"Fors"* xxi)? How am I to account for this discourse other than to consider its summons in light of the Gothic? When Jacques Derrida says "the inhabitant of a crypt is always a living-dead," he is saying nothing new to an entire generation of North American readers and film-goers whose attraction to the horror genre raises various theoretical questions, not the least of which is posed by Noël Carroll who asks

"Why horror?" ... If horror necessarily has something repulsive about it, how can audiences be attracted to it? Indeed, if horror only caused fear, we might feel justified in demanding an explanation of what could motivate people to seek out the genre. But where fear is compounded with repulsion, the ante is, in a manner of speaking, raised. (158)

Indeed, to speculate upon the connections that might be made between the writing of Jacques Derrida and the works of a genre that has long been associated with attraction and repulsion leads one into some strange territory. Although it might be a misnomer to call Jacques Derrida a Gothic novelist (it's tempting though), it would also be a mistake to deny his affinity with the genre since the elements of the Gothic are undeniably present in his work.[16] What do the works of popular culture tell us about Jacques Derrida?

Susan Buck-Morss points out that Walter Benjamin took seriously "the debris of mass culture as the source of philosophical truth" (ix). She claims that Benjamin's goal in the Arcades project was

to take materialism so seriously that the historical phenomena themselves were brought to speech. The project was to test "how 'concrete' one can be in connection with the history of philosophy." Corsets, feather dusters, red and green colored combs, old photographs, souvenir replicas of the Venus di Milo, collar buttons to shirts long discarded – these battered historical survivors from the dawn of the industrial culture that appeared together in the dying arcades as "a world of secret affinities" *were* the philosophical ideas, as a constellation of concrete, historical referents. (3–4)

Buck-Morss's remarks suggest that if these urban objects can draw attention to themselves as a philosophical discourse, then the "objects" of popular culture – arguably the themes, tropes, and topoi of Gothic fiction and film – might give themselves over to being read "as a constellation of concrete, historical referents"[17] that otherwise might be unspeakable.

Thus, when Derrida remarks that "the crypt from which the ghost *comes back* belongs to someone else" (note to "*Fors*" 119), we are given to understand (1)that we are being drawn into the unconscious transmission and reception of "living-dead knowledge" (which is thus, nescience); (2)that we are being drawn into close proximity with that which defies verbalization because it is the *condition* of writing, speaking, *and* being and is untraceable except through its effects. As far as the crypt is concerned, what can "take place" can do so only by *producing* concealment – that is, the (crypt) *effect* of interiority – which is accomplished by "constructing a system of partitions, with their inner and outer surfaces" ("*Fors*" xiv). Derrida, in fact, is everywhere concerned with a certain "beyond place" "non-place" or "no-place" [*non-lieu*] which, he tellingly describes as "the *other* place" (xxi).

Derrida's remarks on the construction of the "cryptic enclave" not only recapitulate Abraham and Torok's notion of the crypt in terms of topography but also recall Eve Kosofsky Sedgwick's assertions regarding the Gothic. Specifically, the structuring of the cryptic enclave, with its ability "to isolate, to protect, to shelter from … penetration" ("*Fors*" xiv) evokes Sedgwick's topographical comments regarding the uncanny and spontaneous production of "strange barriers" which "spring up and multiply" through the formal energy of the Gothic (20). Similarly, Derrida's assertion that the crypt is "*built* by violence" (xv) – and that to penetrate it we must use a certain "break-in technique" (xv) which "consists of locating the crack or the lock, choosing the angle of a partition, and forcing entry" (xv) – recalls Eve Kosofsky Sedgwick's remarks regarding the "extremes of magic or violence" (20) necessary to breach the strange barriers erected in the Gothic. Sedgwick's assertions point to the way that the structuring principle of the Gothic consistently evokes the fantasy of incorporation – including the encryption of libidinal forces. Derrida's comments regarding the psychic apparatus of incorporation suggest that he has found that fantasy efficacious in terms of deconstructive autobiography.[18] When coupled with Sedgwick's comments regarding the structuring principle of the Gothic – predicated upon the production of "strange barriers" which "spring up and multiply" – Derrida's remarks about the crypt suggest the similarities or avenues of correspondence that exist between that principle and the fantasy of incorporation as proposed by Abraham and Torok. It is this correspondence that calls attention to Jacques Derrida's practice of writing *with* ghosts that I call cryptomimesis.

What stands out in Derrida's work is the multiple functioning of the crypt. Firstly, Derrida's designation of "crypt" as a *name* (which is not to be confused with any bearer) leads us into thinking of that which signs, or takes place, *posthumously*. But in order to sign, the name "crypt" needs an equally uncanny structure: the ear of the other. The crypt also designates a place, "a very specific and peculiar place" according to Derrida, who draws our attention to the crypt's structural properties when he says that the crypt houses "the ghost that comes haunting out of the Unconscious of the other" and that "the crypt from which the ghost *comes back* belongs to someone else" (*"Fors"* 119). One could call this return the work of mourning.

Derrida's concerns with the crypt suggest that the phantom figures as the effect of what, although it is barred from conscious-ness, returns to "haunt." Esther Rashkin draws attention to this phenomenon in her discussion of the phantom which, she says, "can 'peregrinate' in several directions and inhabit strangers as well as family members" (10).[19] Herein, the phantom is passed on through generations as a secret that is unspeakable because it is *silenced*. Silence figures heavily in the transmission of the unsayable secret as Nicholas Rand suggests:

Whether it characterizes individuals, families, social groups, or entire nations, silence and its varied forms – the untold or unsayable secret, the feeling unfelt, the pain denied, the unspeakable and concealed shame of families, the cover-up of political crimes, the collective disregard for pain-ful historical realities – may disrupt our lives. (*The Shell and the Kernel* 21)

While these remarks draw attention to the phantom as the silent transmission of a secret, they also suggest a relationship among the phantom, haunting, and writing since each, in its own way, posits

that the return of the dead enacts an inheritance – a "will," perhaps
beyond the grave: a notion that also recalls Derrida's remarks on
writing and iterability beyond the death of the addressee. In other
words, writing, textuality, the phantom, and haunting are not only
interrelated; they are inseparable. To make this assertion is also to
say that writing is phantom-driven and that we all have our ghosts,
a thought that renders classical notions of subjectivity more enigmatic than ever. As Derrida puts it in *Specters of Marx*, "everyone
reads, acts, writes with *his or her* ghosts, even when one goes after
the ghosts of the other" (139).

To write *with* ghosts, however, is to effect a writing practice that
admits the *unheimlich* – the uncanny effect of a certain spacing of
which Derrida says, "it feels itself occupied, in the proper secret ...
of its inside, by what is most strange, distant, threatening" (144–5).
Such a writing would, by necessity, be *cryptic* because it stands on
the border of divulging *and* hiding, remembering *and* forgetting,
producing a curious *fort/da* tension that is, as Deleuze and Guattari
say of writing that deals with the "secret," always "becoming"
(289). In effect, the crypt is a model and a method of producing
concealment or what Heidegger calls *aletheia*. The crypt, therefore,
is not to be thought of merely as a metaphor for the unconscious,
"hidden, secret, underground, [or] latent" nor as a "literal meaning" ("*Fors*" xiii), but rather as a term referring to a writing
practice that takes into account a secret, a tomb, a burial, and a
return – aspects of what Derrida calls "metaphoricity itself."

A writing that is always becoming (secret), then, would proceed
hieroglyphically, as a rebus does, to acquire its own form. This
"form," therefore, would not be static but "most strange, distant
[and] threatening" because it is ceaselessly reconstituted, changing,
multiple, fluid, feminine, but without example! According to
Deleuze and Guattari,

the more the secret is made into a structuring, organizing form, the thinner
and more ubiquitous it becomes, the more its content becomes molecular,
at the same time as its form dissolves. It really wasn't much, as Jocasta
says. The secret does not as a result disappear, but it does take on a more
feminine status. What was behind ... Schreber's paranoid secret all along,
if not a becoming-feminine, a becoming woman? (289)

Derrida's experimentation with the rebus technique – which, as
Gregory Ulmer puts it, amounts to "the reduction of the phonetic

in favor of the ideographic element in writing" (*Applied Grammatology* 71) – has had the effect of raising the possibility that the secret or, better yet, secrecy, functions as the structural enigma which inaugurates the scene of writing. That "scene," in Derrida's terms, "mobilizes various forces, or if you prefer various agencies or 'subjects,' some of which *demand* the narrative of the other, seek to extort it from him, like a secret-less secret" ("Living On – Border Lines" 260). In this scene, writing comes before language. It *produces* differentiation – spacing – in an enigmatic way, the model of which might be understood in terms of dream production, wherein the twin processes of condensation and displacement function in secret to cross the phonetic with the ideographic.[20]

Cryptomimesis or,
the Return of the Living-Dead

Much has already been written about Derrida's "non-linear" writing and his attempts to balance the ideographic with the phonetic elements of writing. Gregory Ulmer's comments best elucidate the range and magnitude of Derrida's efforts:

Grammatology confronts nothing less than the sediment of four thousand years of the history of language, during which time everything that resisted linearization was suppressed. Briefly stated, this suppression amounts to the denial of the pluridimensional character of symbolic thought originally evident in the "mythogram" (Leroi-Gourhan's term), or nonlinear writing (pictographic and rebus writing). In the mythogram, meaning is not subjected to successivity, to the order of logical time, or to the irreversible temporality of sound. The linear schema of unfolding presence, where the line relates the final presence to the originary presence according to the straight line or the circle, became a *model*, Derrida says, and as such became inaccessible and invisible. Given Heidegger's demonstration that this mundane concept of temporality (homogeneous, dominated by the form of the now and the ideal of continuous movement, straight or circular) is the determining concept of all ontology from Aristotle to Hegel, and the assumption that the linearity of language entails just this concept of time, Derrida concludes that "the meditation upon writing and the deconstruction of the history of philosophy become inseparable" (*Applied Grammatology* 8).

Where Ulmer's interest in Derrida's "meditation upon writing" takes the form of what he calls "applied grammatology," my concern is to explore and elaborate upon what I have called Derrida's poetics of the crypt. This phrase draws attention to cryptomimesis as textual production that is predicated upon haunting, mourning, and the return of the so-called living dead. In cryptomimesis, the structuring principle is abjection. Because Derrida's writing resists linearization, it escapes the system of binary logic which would suppress "the pluridimensional character of symbolic thought." In fact, cryptomimesis approaches abjection because it concerns itself with the collapse, or the permeability, of the border between inside and outside, between attraction and repulsion. To this end, the tension between attraction and repulsion generate a writing that might be best thought of in terms of *de/composition*, since that word draws attention not only to death and to the decay that the crypt implies, but also to how cryptomimesis is a writing practice that is characterized by disintegration, by the breaking-up of language into its elements or constituents. Decomposition – and all it implies – might also be thought of as the aesthetic principle behind cryptomimesis which, because it sets up a challenge to "taste," has its affinity with Gothic "horror."

"It is disgust that controls everything," says Derrida in a footnote to "Otobiographies" (23). Although Derrida is commenting on Nietzsche's recognition of the role of disgust in the constitution of institutions, his remarks serve also to suggest a correspondence between his work (Derrida's) and the aesthetics of Gothic horror, the key element of which, asserts Noël Carroll in *The Philosophy of Horror*, is "disgust" (158). While Derrida's writing practice suggests a kinship with Gothic horror in popular culture, a link can also be made between Derrida's aesthetics, stated in architectural terms, and Edgar Allan Poe's "The Fall of the House of Usher." Poe's story alerts us to the crypt as being a poetic device, a discursive effect, as well as a site of disgust in the form of abjection.

But to return, briefly, to the notion of "decomposition": the term gives us to understand what Nicholas Rand means when he discusses "the processes of integrity and simultaneous disintegration Derrida has outlined historically and practiced in his readings over the last twenty years" (*Wolf Man's* lxix). Rand goes on to say:

Understood as an "impossibility to be," disintegration does not counteract the notion of or the fact of integrity. Disintegration is the opaque beyond or far side of apparent integrity inasmuch as integrity (Being) is nothing but the potentially telling and allusive account of why and how something could not be. With this definition of what is, in relation to something beyond that could not be, [we can] situate Derridean deconstruction retroactively as the systematic exploration of fictitious verbal scenarios that articulate obstacles to being. (lxix)

Even though Derrida's writing practice has been described in terms of the rebus technique, I want to shift attention to how the crypt functions in Derrida's work as a poetic *device* that *determines* what Ulmer refers to above as the "pluridimensional character of symbolic thought." The crypt reminds us that Derrida's writing practice is predicated upon "decomposition" which is, as Gregory Ulmer suggests, "another version of what Derrida describes as the most fundamental feature of language – iterability, the principle shared by both speech and writing" (*Applied Grammatology* 58). Ulmer points out that the crucial element of Derrida's de/compositional mode of writing is the grapheme, which remains iterable and, like the mark, may continue "to function *in the absence of its context*" (58). In effect, the crypt serves as a de/compositional principle predicated upon detachment, dissolving, disintegration:

And this is the possibility on which I want to insist [says Derrida]: the possibility of disengagement and citational graft which belongs to the structure of every mark, spoken or written, and which constitutes every mark in writing before and outside of every horizon of semio-linguistic communication; in writing, which is to say in the possibility of its functioning being cut off, at a certain point, from its "original" desire-to-say-what-one-means and from its participation in a saturable and constraining context. Every sign, linguistic or non-linguistic, spoken or written (in the current sense of this opposition), in a small or large unit, can be *cited*, put between quotation marks; in so doing it can break with every given context, engendering an infinity of new contexts in a manner which is absolutely illimitable. ("Signature Event Context" qtd. in Ulmer, *Applied Grammatology* 58–9)[1]

To achieve such a writing, Derrida follows the lead of Abraham and Torok whose "theory of readability" was predicated upon their phonetic analysis of the Wolf Man's dreams which, they argue, are comprised of the combinations of sounds derived from three languages (English, Russian, and German). In the famous wolf dream, for example, Abraham and Torok demonstrate the workings of citation when they demonstrate how the phrase, "It was night" – in Russian, *notchiu* – breaks from its context to slip into the homophonically similar English, "not you" (*Wolf Man's* 34), a shift that demonstrates how the inner workings of the crypt are predicated upon the ear as well as the mouth, which Gregory Ulmer describes as an "organ of [Derrida's] new philosopheme" (*Applied Grammatology* 57) in that the mouth offers "a model for a methodology of decomposition" (57).

In Derrida's work the word "crypt" should always be thought of as being put between quotation marks, which remind us of "teeth" and, therefore, of decomposition, assimilation, and especially, incorporation.[2] In fact, Derrida's remark that "the crypt is the *vault* of a desire" ("*Fors*" xvii) suggests a certain architecture, one that keeps a desire "safe" from assimilation and, therefore, "alive." Encryption involves the production of an architecture that preserves and pays homage to desire, which is why Derrida says of the crypt that it "commemorates ... the exclusion of a specific desire from the introjection process: A door is silently sealed off like a condemned passageway inside the Self, becoming the outcast safe" (xvii). Where the notion of commemoration also suggests a certain funereal practice – let's call it an "undertaking" since Derrida is so fond of that word – it also draws attention to the *dynamics* of a textual production, a kind of writing beyond the grave, that is predicated *not only* upon condensation and displacement, as in dream-writing, but also upon the twin psychic processes of haunting and (the refusal of) mourning which, like dream production, are unconscious processes that exceed the limits of philosophical discourse. Gregory Ulmer points out what is at stake for Derrida:

the model for an unconscious writing – its rationale – is provided by theories devised to explain the language of the Wolf Man, whose compulsive or unconscious condition separating him from his "name," or "signature," makes him a test case for a new theory of writing. Derrida's strategy for exceeding the limits of philosophical discourse is to learn to write the way the Wolf Man spoke. (*Applied Grammatology* 60)

To learn to write the way the Wolf Man spoke is to draw upon the notion of incorporation – the psychic process responsible for the formation of the "crypt." "The model for an unconscious writing

– its rationale – [says Ulmer] is provided by theories devised to explain the language of the Wolf Man, whose compulsive or unconscious condition [separated] him from his 'name' or 'signature'" (60). Although Abraham and Torok's reading of the Wolf Man's dreams provides Derrida with a strategy for writing, Derrida does not concur with their notion that incorporation is a *pathology* inhibiting mourning. Rather, the fantasy of incorporation is understood by Derrida as an inhibition *necessary* for the very possibility of the "subject." Thus, "to learn to write the way the Wolf Man spoke" is to do the work of refused mourning, which is cryptomimesis.

A PROBLEM OF SPACING:
BEHIND THE DOOR IS INSIDE MYSELF

The work of mourning requires that a space be created within the self so that the other can be assimilated, digested, made part of us. That "self," nevertheless, is constituted only in relationship to an other who is never assimilated but who *necessarily* remains other, outside, over-there, never to be "devoured." Paradoxically, it is only in bereavement that this "self," referred to by Derrida as a "specular reflection," appears. Says Derrida, "it does not appear *before* [the] *possibility* of mourning" ("Mnemosyne" 28). A paradox ensues because, as one reader has found, "the condition for the possibility of mourning is the condition for its impossibility" (Bracken 225). Christopher Bracken elucidates the paradox, explaining, "it is mourning which establishes the enclosure where the other is held in the work of mourning. Since mourning builds up the self where mourning unfolds, it has to occur in advance of itself if it is to happen at all. But that is impossible" (225).

It is only by grieving for another who has yet to die – the *anticipation* of mourning – that, says Derrida, "all 'being-in-us,' 'in me,' 'between us', or between ourselves" is constituted in advance ("Mnemosyne" 28). It is the *possibility* of death, therefore, that determines the "within-me" and the "within-us." With this in mind, Freud's axiom might then be re-written: profound mourning is the reaction to the [anticipated] loss of someone who is loved.

But what happens when mourning is refused? Although Derrida's remarks on mourning demonstrate the paradox implicit in the so-called normal work of mourning, they also give us to understand how the necessary relation of Being to the law is determined by the equally necessary "failure" to mourn, otherwise known as incorporation, a process which denotes a *fantasy*. Referred to by Maria Torok in *The Shell and the Kernel* as a "fantasmic mechanism," ("The Illness of Mourning" 113) incorporation is distinct from introjection (a gradual process), in that it signals the "failure" or the "refusal" to digest or assimilate the other. If the dead other is not to be interiorized, it is, nonetheless, taken inside the subject and lodged within the ego, but as a secret, sealing the loss of the object and marking the refusal to mourn. Incorporation marks the limits of introjection since it consists of the desire (whose?) to keep the dead *alive*, safe, inside me.

But how can the dead live inside me? Where would they find "lodging"? Abraham and Torok use the concept of the crypt to designate a unique intrapsychic topography which inexpressible mourning erects inside the subject as a secret tomb which houses the idealized dead other as living. They see the crypt as a formation constituted through the fantasy of incorporation, which simulates introjection. Two interrelated procedures comprise the "magic" of incorporation: "*demetaphorization* (taking literally what is meant figuratively) and *objectivation* (pretending that the suffering is not an injury to the subject but instead a loss sustained by the love object)" ("Mourning *or* Melancholia" 126–7). In "Mourning *or* Melancholia," Abraham and Torok describe the crypt's structure:

Reconstituted from the memories of words, scenes, and affects, the objectal correlative of the loss is buried alive in the crypt as a full-fledged person, complete with its own topography. The crypt also includes the actual or supposed traumas that made introjection impracticable. A whole world of unconscious fantasy is created, one that leads its own separate and concealed existence. Sometimes in the dead of night, when libidinal fulfillments have their way, the ghost of the crypt comes back to haunt the cemetery guard. (130)

The ghost comes back because what is buried is untellable and, therefore, (necessarily) inaccessible to the gradual, painful, assimilative work of mourning. Derrida is careful to point out an aporia in the thinking about the "'normal' 'work of mourning'" which, he says, "since Freud," has been based upon the notion of "interiorizing idealization" and assimilation – "possible" mourning, in other words – to the exclusion of anticipated mourning as a prior structure enabling the "me" or the "us" ("Mnemosyne" 34). It is with this structure – cryptic incorporation – in mind that crypto-mimesis performs the (impossible) work of mourning because it is concerned with "the *unreadability* of mourning" (34).

According to Freud, "profound mourning" is the "reaction to the loss of someone who is loved" ("Mourning and Melancholia" 244). Freud also claims that "the work which mourning performs" consists of a long, slow, and "painful" withdrawal of the attachments which connect us to the loved one who has died (244). Withdrawal of attachments, moreover, is accomplished only through prolonged memory work which, says Derrida, "entails a movement in which an interiorizing idealization takes in itself or upon itself the body and voice of the other, the other's visage and person, ideally *and* quasi-literally devouring them" ("Mnemosyne" 34). An interior-izing idealization then concludes the work of mourning through an act of *assimilation* – an introjection – which, through what Derrida calls, "faithful interiorizaton," expands the self. The fantasy of cryptic incorporation differs from introjection in that the lost object is not assimilated but is sustained in some way. This is cryptomimesis.

Judith Butler draws attention to the difference between introjec-tion and incorporation in her discussion of melancholy, "which denotes a *magical* resolution of loss," versus mourning:

Abraham and Torok suggest that introjection of the loss characteristic of mourning establishes *an empty space*, literalized by the empty mouth which becomes the condition of speech and signification. The successful displacement of the libido from the lost object is achieved through the formation of *words* which both signify and displace that object; this displacement from the original object is an essentially metaphorical activity in which words "figure" the absence and surpass it... Whereas introjection founds the possibility of metaphorical signification, incorporation is anti-metaphorical precisely because it maintains the loss as radically unname-able; in other words, incorporation is not only a failure to name or avow the loss, but erodes the conditions of metaphorical signification itself. (*Gender Trouble* 68)

It is apparent in Butler's remarks that she, like Abraham and Torok, considers the fantasy of incorporation – that is, the refusal of loss or melancholia – in terms of a certain psychopathology. Derrida, on the other hand, sees incorporation as the *possibility* of the subject, which is how Mark Wigley describes Derrida's re-thinking of the subject in terms of the crypt (176). Wigley suggests that "the subject is constructed as such by the spacing of the crypt. It's therefore not just that the crypt is the desired effect of Derrida's texts or even that the crypt is always an effect of desire. More than the maintenance of a forbidden desire, the crypt is the very figure of desire" (176). It becomes clear, therefore, that Derrida considers that haunting, the phantom, and the crypt are always already the very condition of the subject. In terms of cryptomimesis, the subject is a crypt-effect of the text, the spectre of desire.

Abraham and Torok also designate the figure of the phantom to draw attention to what they call the "shadow of the object." This, they say, comes back to haunt by being "reincarnated in the person of the subject" (The Lost Object – Me," 141). In cryptomimesis, the moment of uncanniness is brought about through the shadow-effect of the other, a textual figure of desire that, in Abraham and Torok's terms, "*carries the ego as its mask*, that is, either the ego itself or some other façade" (141).[3] Derrida infers this *unheimlich* shadow structure in "Otobiographies" when he comments, "the ear is uncanny. Uncanny is what it is; double is what it can become" (33). Where the phantom indicates a rift in the ego, it returns to haunt its host through a mechanism which, according to Abraham and Torok, "consists of exchanging one's own identity for a fantasmic identification with the 'life' – beyond the grave – of an object of love" ("The Lost Object – Me" 142). Although it takes many forms in endocryptic identification, "the 'I,'" say Abraham and Torok, "is understood as the lost *object's fantasied ego*" (148, emphasis mine) who haunts the subject through a kind of *ventriloquism*. The writer of "Envois" plays upon this art of speaking as if the voice appears to come from some source *other* than the speaker:

In your name you are my destiny, for me you are destiny. Everything began, you remember, when I pronounced it, you had your hands on the wheel, and I know that I am writing this, my destiny, fate, my chance, when on the envelope I *risk*, which is indeed how I feel the thing, when I risk the first word of the address. I address myself to you, somewhat as if I were sending my self, never certain of seeing it come back, that which is destined for me. And when I am able to pronounce it, when I softly call myself by your name, nothing else is there, do you hear, nothing else, no one else in the world. Even us perhaps and yes our existence is threatened then. (45)

As the speaker implies, the oscillations between "self" and "other" are precarious. A risk is involved in sending the "Envois" since it is death that lies between the two. Indeed, the speaker appears to find him(?)self occupied by the (phantom of the) other, whose absence, nevertheless, opens the space for writing:

I ask myself occasionally quite simply if you exist and if you have the slightest notion of it.

No literature with this, not with you my love. Sometimes I tell myself that you are my love: then it is only my love, I tell myself interpellating myself thus. And then you no longer exist, you are dead, like the dead woman in my game, and my literature becomes possible. (29)

In the "Envois," the phantom returns to haunt because it must signify the loss which is the result of refused mourning. In this sense, what "speaks" in the "Envois" is writing itself, already occupied by the other: "You give me words, you deliver them, dispensed one by one my own, while turning them toward yourself and addressing them to yourself" (12).

Comprised of "subjects" who, like Poe's Roderick Usher, feel themselves haunted, the "Envois" openly admit the *unheimlich* through vertiginous shiftings between the distinctions of "inside" and "outside." In these terms *to be* is to be *haunted*, if not by the dead, then by what Nicholas Rand refers to as "their lives' unfinished business [that] is unconsciously handed down to their descendants" (*The Shell and the Kernel* 167). The writer of the letter dated 4 June 1977 brings this notion forward:

Have you seen this card, the image on the back [*dos*] of this card? I stumbled across it yesterday, in the Bodleian (the famous Oxford library), I'll tell you about it. I stopped dead, with a feeling of hallucination (is he crazy or what? he has the names mixed up!) and of revelation at the same time, an apocalyptic revelation: Socrates writing, writing in front of Plato, I always knew it, it had remained like the negative of a photograph to be developed for twenty-five centuries – in me, of course. ("Envois" 9)

As the "Envois" suggest, the idea of the phantom and haunting have implications beyond individual or even familial psychology since the concept of haunting generates the potential for inquiry into the advent of social institutions. Because this concept may, as Nicholas Rand suggests, "provide a new perspective for inquiring into the ... roots of cultural patterns and political ideology" (*The Shell* 169), it also has the potential to generate writing that, to use Derrida's term, "refuses itself to philosophy" ("A 'Madness'" 347).

DEPARTED IS THE SUBJECT

The theory of the phantom (along with the crypt and the effects of mourning and haunting) has particular resonance when it comes to theorizing cryptomimesis. It draws our attention to Derrida's efforts to show that the mode of being of the literary work of art is analogous to how a certain "subjectivity" is predicated upon mechanisms of haunting and mourning. Likewise, the theory of the phantom demonstrates how writing takes the form of a displacement that is necessarily cryptically structured by a refusal of mourning which, again, finds its analogy in the (future) possibility of the subject. Derrida's reply to the question "why is it so important to write" suggests what is at stake here: "the self does not exist, it is not present to itself before that which engages it in this way and which is not it. There is not a constituted subject that engages itself at a given moment in writing for some reason or another. It is *given* by writing, by the other" ("A 'Madness'" 347). In these terms, to undertake a piece of work is to do the work of mourning which, in cryptomimesis, demands that one put into practice what Derrida calls in "Cartouches" a "theory of coffins" (186).

A theory of coffins draws attention to the function of a crypt (that is, to house the remains of the dead) and also to everything that the crypt implies, especially in terms of the Gothic: inheritance, haunting, mourning. In the Gothic the crypt implies the revenant, the ghost, and haunting. Derrida's work intersects with that of the Gothic when it comes to the subject of haunting. And to introduce the *subject* of haunting is, of course, to go to the heart of cryptomimesis. When Derrida writes in "Cartouches," "*departed* is the subject" (190) he is not only binding together various strands of thought that go into the deconstruction of presence and of "consciousness," but also alluding to a writing practice that might, paradoxically, be called posthumous and therefore "post-Derridean," for it evokes his own notion that for the written to be the written, it must continue to "act" and to be legible even if what is called the author of the writing no longer answers for what he has written, for what he seems to have signed, whether he is provisionally absent, or if he is dead, or if in general he does not support, with his absolutely current and present intention or attention, the plenitude of his meaning, of that very thing which seems to be written "in his name." ("Signature Event Context" 91)

For writing to continue to "act," it must do so from beyond the grave; that is, it "comes back." In this sense all writing, says Derrida, if it is to be "iterable," "must be able to function in the radical absence of every empirically determined addressee in general. And this absence is not a continuous modification of presence; it is a break in presence, 'death,' or the possibility of the 'death' of the addressee, inscribed in the structure of the mark" (91). Thus, to say "departed is the subject," is to allude to what makes writing possible: death, or a break in presence.

It is also to suggest what is at stake in a writing that, in this case, draws attention to itself grammatically as a sentence predicated (if this can be the word) upon the *dislocation* of the sense of being that, in terms of logocentrism, is tied to what Derrida calls in *Of Grammatology*, "the precomprehension of the *word being*" (21). The subject of logocentrism, as Derrida makes abundantly clear, is an effect of language or, better yet, of the linear sentence. This linear model is one way of understanding what Derrida means when he says that Western metaphysics and thus presence "is produced as the domination of a linguistic form" (40). It is the linear model (the subject-predicate and the present indicative of the verb "to be") that produces both the "subject" and meaning in unfolding presence, which is why to write, "departed is the subject" is to suggest that the subject is instead a phantom structure – as in the "departed" – and also that writing is necessarily marked by departure, by leave-taking, and by death.

To write, thus, is *to anticipate the memory of one's other*; one's departed. The word "departed," which has its roots in the Latin *dispertire*, to divide, reminds us of Derrida's assertion that writing has "a possibility of functioning *cut off*, at a certain point, from its 'original' meaning and from its belonging to a saturable and constraining context" ("Signature Event Context" 97, italics mine). Similarly, linking the notion of departure with that of one's other recalls Derrida's remarks regarding the ear of the other which, he says, is "double." To write "departed is the subject" is to bring forward the notion of haunting, for it is not enough merely to claim that the transcendental signifier of "God" or the "author" is "dead": the undoing of (the subject of) logocentrism/phonocentrism/ontotheology is never absolute. One can't help but wonder – if (it is) God (who) is dead, (why) does He continue to haunt? While the question seems unresolvable, it might be better addressed if one considers the paradox in the dream, reported by Freud in *The Interpretation of Dreams*, about the father who does not know he is dead: "[the dreamer's] father was alive once more and was talking to him in his usual way, but (the remarkable thing was that) he was nevertheless dead, only he did not know it" (430). Later, as Jane Gallop observes, Lacan will point out just how ambiguous the pronoun *he* really is (*Reading Lacan* 157–85).

What returns to haunt is what remains of a certain structure. Call it the third person singular of the present indicative through which *being* is understood. Although, as Heidegger points out, "we explain the infinitive to be to ourselves through the is" (*An Introduction to Metaphysics* 92), the "Envois" demonstrate what happens when that verb form is displaced by that which is forever absent. Yet *to be* cannot be dispensed with completely, which is one reason why Derrida remarks in *Of Grammatology* that one "cannot *criticize* metaphysics radically without still utilizing [it] in a certain way" (19). To utilize metaphysics "in a certain way" is not "to attempt a step outside metaphysics" (for there is no "outside") but rather to inhabit it – or better yet to haunt it – within a gesture of displacement made possible though the crypt. Such a displacement puts metaphysics under erasure because, as Derrida remarks, it "obeys a different *trop*ography" ("*Fors*" xiii). While Derrida's thematizing of the crypt is often apparent, the more important and less apparent challenge of cryptomimesis is to devise a mode of thought that undermines what Gayatri Spivak refers to as a "longing for a center, an authorizing pressure" (lxix). In cryptomimesis this is accomplished through a writing "that takes the form of everything a crypt implies: *topoi, death, cipher*" ("*Fors*" xiii). The function of such a displacement is to induce the reader to do memory work, which is also dream-work that encourages what Derrida refers to as "an entire thematics of active interpretations, which substitutes an incessant deciphering for the disclosure of truth as a presentation of the thing itself."[4]

Cryptomimesis invites interminable analysis in that it is a kind of writing that is self-referential yet co-exists in a relation of correspondence with other writing. It is a dream of language that produces an uncanny tropography similar to that of the Gothic novel in that it seems to turn upon what Eve Sedgwick calls the "half-submerged association [between dreaming and language] that occurs in Gothic novels when a dream is ... described as 'unspeakable' or the past ... as 'buried'" (62). Cryptomimesis is, in short, a burial practice that, like incorporation, preserves desire, keeping it alive in a complex architecture: "the love-object (in phantasy life) is walled up or entombed and thus preserved as a bit of the outside inside the inside, kept apart from the 'normal' introjections of the Self" (Ulmer, *Applied Grammatology* 61). To entomb the object is to keep it preserved, alive "inside the inside," kept "apart." Again, this is why Derrida calls the crypt, "the vault of desire."

Derrida's remarks suggest that a crypt, like a rebus, is marked by cross-currents of desire that are productive for, in this case, a "vault" is not only architectural – a dome, ceiling, arch, or safe – it is also performative, since it suggests the "mounting" of desire as well as the function of the crypt which is to keep safe the contradictory demands "springing" from incorporation. Says Derrida, "*To crypt*: I do not think I have yet used it as a verb. To crypt is to cipher, a symbolic or semiotic operation that consists of manipulating a secret code, which is something one can never do alone ... [Cryptic operation involves] verbal machinery or machinations, often lexical or even nominal. A machine, yes, and a calculating shrewdness" ("*Fors*" xxxvi–vii). To crypt is characteristically Gothic. The dynamic structure brings forward what Sedgwick, in her discussion of Gothic themes, calls "a relation of correspondence" (40) Here, "correspondence" is "distinguished from direct communication, which is seen as impossible; instead it moves by a relation of counterparts and doubles, and is subject to dangerous distortions and interferences" (40). A cryptomimetic machine moves by a similar relation of "counterparts and doubles," asking of its reader, a similar, singular affirmation: *yes*, (a) crypt, but how to get into it? Since there are always ghosts in the machine, engaging in a cryptic operation requires a "calculating shrewdness." This shrewdness is perhaps what Lorraine Weir has in mind in her approach to reading Joyce's cryptic operations, a task very much like reading Derrida's. This process, says Weir, requires

not passive submission on our part but, rather, engagement in its processing. Thus not a conversion, not a permanent transcoding operation, but the demand placed on the listener by complex music, the willingness to be programmed, to enter into processually governed expectation, anticipation, and resolution. Our task, to rearrange ourselves "in" the system, is initially a theological one. But where is "inside"? If to process the system is not to stand "outside" its semantic claims, then how do we approach the task of standing "inside" it? (3)

How, indeed, to "arrange" ourselves in what Weir calls a "performance system" when cryptomimesis evokes what might be thought of as the "dizziness of mind" referred to by Paul de Man in his discussion of the poetic sign's capacity to "set in motion an imaging activity that refers to *no object in particular*" ("The Dead-End of Formalist Criticism" 236). And de Man was not even talking about a crypt! In cryptomimesis, the "imaging activity" can be understood as the *work* of the phantom but, strictly speaking, the phantom *cannot be thought* since haunting implies a return only of that which is *unthinkable*.

THE NAME OF THE NOT

In analysis, bringing the phantom to light is difficult since, according to Nicolas Abraham, "the phantoms inhabiting our minds do so without our knowledge" ("The Intermission of 'Truth'" 188). The task is no less difficult in textual analysis, for, as in the psyche, phantoms dwell in secret, encrypted in the unconscious, manifesting in the very nature of "what returns to haunt, in the nature of the thing 'phantomized'" (189). Whether one is speaking of psychoanalysis or text analysis, bringing the phantom to light is difficult not only because the process of transference is at work, but because the crypt from which the phantom returns, and which is lodged in "my" unconscious, might well belong to the preceding generation. Reading for the "phantom" becomes even more difficult since what is "phantomized," according to Nicolas Abraham, is wrapped in silence "because it was unspeakable in words" (189).

Whether in psychoanalysis or text analysis, what is phantomized or encrypted is passed on as an (unconscious) inheritance. This idea of an unconscious legacy unsettles any classical notions of the subject, the unconscious, and for that matter, "autobiography," since the theory of the phantom suggests that the "I" with which one speaks also functions as the crypt out of which the ghost returns. Derrida remarks on this complex structure when, in "Roundtable on Autobiography," he refers to an analysis of Nietzsche's "ghost" which, Derrida suggests, could be undertaken in the general space where Nietzsche implies, "I am my father and my mother ... I am their crypt and they both speak to me. They both speak in me so whatever I say, they address it to each other" (58–9). Whether in psychoanalysis or text analysis, Derrida's use of the word "address" to describe the crypt's effect is significant because it links the crypt, the phantom, haunting, and inheritance to writing and sending. These "correspondences" which determine the *effects* of the crypt in the unconscious of a subject or a text can be thought of in terms of what Derrida, in "Envois" calls "postality": "postal maneuvering, relays, delay, anticipation, destination, telecommunicating network, the possibility, and therefore the fatal necessity of going astray, etc." (66). The notion of "postal maneuvering" reminds us of the possibility that what is sent out will never arrive at its destination, but also of the likelihood that what is sent out is unconscious in that it is, as Lacan would say, the discourse of the other that is, as Derrida would add, yet to come. This possibility becomes apparent in Derrida's reference to writing as an "enigma of a truth *to be made*" ("A 'Madness'" 347). Although this idea has implications for both psychoanalysis and text analysis, it suggests that what the two have in common is the postal system. What makes analysis difficult in either case is the crypt. In "Roundtable on Autobiography," Derrida refers explicitly to such difficulty:

When it's a text that one is trying to decipher or decrypt using [Abraham and Torok's theory of the crypt], or when one is looking for a ghost or a crypt in a text, then things get still more difficult, or let us say more novel. I say a ghost *and* a crypt: actually the theory of the "ghost" is not exactly the theory of the "crypt." It's even more complicated. Although it's also connected to the crypt, the ghost is more precisely the effect of another's crypt in my unconscious. (59)

To say that things get more "novel" when one is looking for a ghost or a crypt in a text draws attention to the dynamics of transference that necessarily exist between a text that cannot set limits to the way it will be read and postality. It is difficult, perhaps impossible, to look for a ghost or a crypt in a text because, although they are figures of *return*, the ghost and the crypt are, themselves, the condition of textuality in general that is yet to come.

Because the ghost and the crypt are conditions of textuality, they are necessarily "unspeakable in words." One could argue, therefore, that the effect of another's crypt in the unconscious implies certain spatial determinants, although it eludes the distinctions between either/or. In a certain way, the theory of the crypt evokes what Mark Taylor refers to as "the not." According to Taylor, the not "falls *between* being and non-being" (1). The "not," of course, has been variously named: "God, Satan, the good, evil, being, nonbeing, absolute knowledge, nonknowledge, the unconscious," (1) and now, perhaps, the phantom. But what's in a name? While the name "God" might be a name for the unnameable, it is also, Taylor suggests "the name that makes the *disappearance* of the name appear. 'God,' then, might be the name for that in language which does not properly belong to language. If it were a name that does not name, the name 'God' might, in a certain sense, be a name for the unnameable ... the unnameable that *haunts* language as a strange exteriority 'within' discourse" (11). Both Weir and Taylor evoke a certain spatial model of language that shows how distinctions between "interiority" and "exteriority" also have theological implications. However, where Taylor differs from Weir, focusing on Derrida's affinity with the Gothic, is in his evocation of *haunting* as the uncanny condition of language, which in turn implies textuality and postality. Taylor's remarks draw attention to the working of a structuring principle that, in cryptomimesis, can be thought of as the "cryptic enclave" produced by virtue of refused mourning ("*Fors*" xiv). Similarly, Taylor's assertion that what haunts language exists as "a strange exteriority 'within' discourse" evokes the fantasy of incorporation that, in the first place, produces the cryptic enclave as an answer to loss.

Like the crypt, the strange topography of language hides and hold the unnameable. The lost object (of desire) haunts only because, by necessity, it was not properly buried/introjected. In effect, the crypt "reveals" language as haunted architecture which, appears to Mark Wigley as "the irrepressible haunting of space, the spectral economy of the haunted house ... [This economy] underpins Derrida's work without ever being its apparent subject, is first and foremost the enigmatic movements of displacement or dislocation" (177). Given the workings of the crypt, these "enigmatic movements of displacement or dislocation," make it difficult for a reader to situate herself "inside" what Derrida himself refers to as the "dizzying topography" of the "crypt." The region of the crypt offers the reader such unstable ground because it draws us into an encounter with writing that, in Nicholas Rand's words (he is referring to the Wolf Man's writing), "resolves the following dilemma: how to live without having to say yes or no to reality or fiction while continuing to refer to both" (*Wolf Man's* lviii).

Although referring to Freud's most famous analysand, Rand's comments regarding Sergei Panokov – better known as the Wolf Man – illuminate Derrida's wish to learn to write the way the Wolf Man spoke. According to Rand, the Wolf Man "could not acquire an identity, be it sexual or psychological, unless he found some *device* for the suspension of the positional properties of language, that is, of its capacity to distinguish true from false and determine value" (lix, emphasis mine). Moreover, claim Abraham and Torok, the Wolf Man "appeared to be two separate people in one, without either of them representing the basic identity of the Wolf Man" (3). In the first instance, the "device" to which Rand refers is, of course, the crypt, the psychic mechanism posited by Abraham and Torok to be the Wolf Man's invention – a "false Unconscious: the crypt in the Ego" (*Wolf Man's* lxxi) – the purpose of which is to conceal and preserve the scene of a seduction. Secondly, such a mechanism enables the scene of seduction to continue to signify unbeknownst to Sergei Panokov at a conscious level; hence, the appearance of "cohabitation, at the [Wolf Man's] core" by his sister and his father, each "distinct from him" (3). What then, does it mean for Derrida to want to learn to write the way the Wolf Man spoke since, in Derrida's work, what is produced is the coming of the other as a *textual effect*?

The matter is not one of identification. In fact, Abraham and Torok posit that the so-called Wolf Man might just as well have been an effect of *Freud's* reading. Similarly, they posit the necessity for a "new conceptual apparatus" based upon "translation" of "established text" resulting in an "invented" text (*Wolf Man's* lxxii).

This remark demonstrates not only that the Wolf Man, as referred to by Abraham and Torok, and by Derrida, is an invention based upon translation. It also raises the question posed by Christie McDonald of "how to think about the relationship of an empirical, individual life to the structure of the written text" (ix). Although the Wolf Man writes, as Derrida says of Nietzsche, "with his name and in his name," describing how he has become what he is, meaning is structurally deferred in his text, until a reader "allies with him and *countersigns* in his or her name" (McDonald, ix). In this way, classical notions of autobiography are undermined for, as McDonald writes,

the *autos*, the self as the subject of biography is displaced into the *otos*, the structure of the ear as perceiving organ so that [according to Derrida] "it is the ear of the other that signs." This means, among other things, that text does not fully control its interpretation; nor can any single reading preempt the field of readings. Both the text and its interpretations remain plural. (ix)

In these terms, the crypt and the ear are inextricably implicated. This is one reason, among many, why reading for the so-called Wolf Man or, for that matter, for "Freud" or "Derrida" is as difficult and as indeterminate as looking for a ghost or a crypt in a text. I am reminded here of comments made in a footnote by Derrida in *The Post Card*, with regard to the signing of his proper name:

I regret that you [*tu*] do not very much trust my signature, on the pretext that we might be several. This is true, but I am not saying so in order to make myself more important by means of some supplementary authority. And even less in order to disquiet, I know what this costs. You are right, doubtless we are several, and I am not as alone as I sometimes say I am when the complaint escapes from me, or when I still put everything into seducing you. ("Envois" 6)

Certainly the difficulties of reading for "Derrida" are addressed in this passage. To whom is it addressed? From whom? In most cases, Derrida's reader will find that Nicholas Rand's remarks with regard to the "Wolf Man" aptly describe "Jacques Derrida": "the Wolf Man is a collection of poetic devices, a compendium of rhymes, puns, silent distortions, and secret verbal contortions" (*Wolf Man's* lvii). To speak of seduction is one thing. But to speak in a polyphonic voice is another, because it recalls Derrida's assertion that "the crypt ... belongs to *someone else*" (note 21, "*Fors*" 119); a crypt is "the lodging, the haunt of a host of ghosts" ("*Fors*" xxiii).[5]

While this remark returns us to the persistence of the dead, it also lends itself to a telling of the other which is writing. Indeed, "Derrida," like the "Wolf Man," is plural – "a collection of poetic devices," etc. "Derrida," like the "Wolf Man," is (a text) always already plurally occupied, in a word, haunted by the inhabitants of a crypt who, as Derrida himself knows, speak, through ventriloquism, "from a topography foreign to the subject" (note 21, "*Fors*" 119). We can hear confirmation of this uncanny state of affairs when in "Envois" we read,

I truly believe that I am singing someone who is dead and that I did not know. I am not singing for the dead (this is the truth according to Genet), I am singing a death, *for* a dead man or woman already [*déjà*]. Although since the gender and number remain inaccessible for me I can always play on the plural. And multiply the example or working hypotheses, the hypotheses of mourning.[6] (143)

To "sing" a death is also to sign a death, to save (*fors*) the inner heart, encrypted and encrypting both interiority and exteriority – the [folds of the] hypotheses of mourning. From a theory of coffins to a poetics of the crypt, a s/cryptic practice which returns to thought, through the refusal of mourning, to thinking, the excluded *unheimlich* – a ghost writing that signs in the ear of the other.

WHO WOULD BE ABLE TO READ IT?

The eye by which I see God is the same eye by which
he sees me.

Angelus Silesius

In Derrida's work, the crypt functions multiply. A conceptual apparatus, it simultaneously illuminates (a text) while it anticipates (an/other). Specifically, in the process, it creates what Roland Barthes refers to as a "scriptor" who is "born simultaneously" with the text and who is "in no way equipped with a being preceding or exceeding the writing" (145). Among the issues that this theoretical position addresses is the reduction of a text/literature to biography, along with the perception that literary works are "expressions" of the author's mind. These perspectives lead not only to biographical criticism but also to the perception of the author as the voice of a single person, perhaps a "Great Man," who is "confiding" in us (143). What Barthes asserts is that "it is language that speaks, not the author" (143). This remark reflects Barthes's contention that the author is an ideological construct of logical positivism and is, in fact, an illusion rooted in empiricism's insistence on "experience" as the source of knowledge, a notion that the theory of the phantom and the crypt has consistently called into question. Barthes proposes that removing the "Author" from the text is to remove limitations that close writing. Instead, Barthes asserts that the author is a function of the text, produced simultaneously with its writing. Barthes also contends that writing is performative and that since the writing of the text takes place in the "here and now," the reader also becomes the writer which is, again, another function of writing. Thus, in Derrida's terms, the ear of the other and the crypt are performatives: textual structures (of desire) that also bring forward the uncanniness implicit in Barthes's propositions in that they bring into the picture the performativity of mourning and haunting. To crypt, therefore, implies translation, the invention of a text that is nevertheless tied to another which is living on as a condition of that invention.

This performativity is consistently in evidence in Derrida's engagement with Heidegger's texts. Heidegger's essay, "The Thing," for example, appears to live on in Derrida's essay, "*Fors*," which displaces, yet saves Heidegger's notion of thingness. In "*Fors*," the theory of the crypt brings forward the fantasy of incorporation implicit in Heidegger's essay "The Thing." Derrida implies this correspondence when, in "*Fors*," his question "What is a crypt?" echoes Heidegger's interrogative, "What is the jug?" Whereas Heidegger's attempts to come to terms with his own question draw attention to the difficulty implicit in challenging what Derrida calls "the very form of the [instituting] question" of philosophy (*Of Grammatology* 19), Derrida demonstrates in "*Fors*" that the "ti esti" (or "what is?") is, like the subject who utters it, a crypt effect of language:

What is a crypt? No crypt presents itself. The grounds ... are so disposed as to disguise and to hide: something, always a body in some way. But also to disguise the act of hiding and to hide the disguise: the crypt [like Heidegger's "jug"?] *hides as it holds* ... A crypt is never natural through and through, and if, as is well, known, *physis* has a tendency to encrypt (itself), that is because it overflows its own bounds and encloses, naturally, its other, all others. (xiv)

Derrida's remarks suggest that he is using the crypt to describe the workings of what he calls elsewhere the strategy of "*sous rature.*" In "*Fors,*" for example, Derrida's assertion that the crypt forms an "enclosure" that functions "to purloin *the thing* from the rest" (xiv) seems not only to recall Poe's "letter" but also to be echoed in Gayatri Spivak's discussion of *sous rature,* which she perceives as a "gesture effacing the presence of a thing and yet keeping it legible" (xli). This is certainly the case with Derrida's reading-writing in general, and of his reading-writing of Heidegger, in particular. The point is that "Derrida" comes about through his reading (incorporation) of "Heidegger," a text that incited Derrida to countersign. This is one reason why Derrida claims, "I almost always write in response to solicitations or provocations" ("This Strange Institution" 41).

In Derrida's work, the crypt is a textual device enabling words to point to at least two different things at the same time. The effect is a complex and paradoxical textual structure that extends an invitation to the reader to learn how to countersign. While that invitation might be understood as learning to write the way the Wolf Man spoke, it can also be understood in terms of solicitation and provocation. This is why, according to Derrida, reading-writing is "something one can never do alone," because the structure of the crypt always implies an *other,* a revenant that is yet to come. As to the question, "Who would be able to read [this writing]," (74) Derrida's answer is telling:

there is no pre-given response. By definition the reader does not exist. Not before the work and as its straightforward "receiver." The dream ... concerns what is in the work which produces its reader, a reader who doesn't yet exist, whose competence cannot be identified, a reader who would be "formed," "trained," instructed, constructed, even engendered, let's say *invented* by the work. Invented, which is to say both found by chance and produced by research. The work then becomes an institution forming its own readers, giving them a competence which they did not possess before: a university, a seminar, a colloquium, a curriculum, a *course*. If we trusted the current distinction between competence and performance, we would say that the work's performance produces or institutes, forms or invents, a new competence for the reader or the addressee who thereby becomes a countersignatory. It teaches him or her, *if s/he is willing*, to countersign. ("This Strange Institution" 74)

To be willing to countersign, we must conclude that instead of containing or reflecting experience, language produces it. To this end, cryptomimesis enters the scene when it is no longer a question of imitation but one of invention. Similarly, cryptomimesis demonstrates that writing is no longer a question of communication, but of participation. Gregory Ulmer's comments regarding the language of the Wolf Man suggest what is at stake in terms of representation in learning to countersign:

The cryptonymy of verbal material that the Wolf Man derived from his fetish scene (the maid on her knees scrubbing the floor, invested as a sign of the primal scene) did not operate by the usual procedures of representation – the symbolizing or hiding of one word behind another, or one thing by a word or a word by a thing. Rather, his names were generated by picking out from the extended series of "allosemes" – the catalogue of uses available for a given word – a particular usage, which is then translated into a synonym (creating thus even greater distance from the secret name). The path from crypt to speech may follow either semantic or phonic paths, with the play between homonyms and synonyms being part of the mechanism ... The linkage of the uttered word to the secret name is so tortuous, a relay-labyrinth of [what Derrida describes as] "non-semantic associations, purely phonetic combinations." (*Applied Grammatology* 62–3)

To foreground Derrida's evocation of the crypt, the phantom and the (return of the) living-dead – tropes and topoi that have been consistently used by Derrida to demonstrate how "all ontologization, all semanticization – philosophical, hermeneutical or pschyoanalytical" (*Specters* 9) are the (bodily) remains of the dead – is to trace the "relay-labyrinth(ine)" design of cryptomimesis. It is to explore the notion that Derrida's compositional mode participates in the *production* of the "fundamental fantasy" of contemporary mass culture by evoking the living-dead as performative, uncanny textual structures. Cryptomimesis lends itself to a thinking of Derrida's (compositional) break with traditional "mimesis," which when linked to "the concept of nature," is in "the service of ... ontotheological humanism" ("Economimesis" 6), including the values and assumptions of realism. It also lends itself to a thinking of the uncanny aspects of Derrida's *poetics* – how to write *with* ghosts – a poetics which exists in a certain relationship of "correspondence" with the Gothic.

"'*Darling*,' it said":
Making a Contract
with the Dead

We go to the School of the Dead to hear a little of what
we are unable to say.

Hélène Cixous (*Three Steps on the Ladder of Writing* 53)

While the workings of cryptomimesis can be thought through
Derrida's theory of coffins, the crypt's tripartite economy of desire,
indebtedness, and haunting can also be approached through Gothic
texts which, through their evocation of the "disgusting," give one
the sense of what, in cryptomimesis, works to abolish representative
distance. Since they explore the contractual aspects implicit in the
return of the dead from the grave, Gothic texts also trace the uncanny
relationship that Derrida evokes between writing and the living-dead
and demonstrate that what is disgusting actually prevents mourning
because it is "unassimilable" ("Economimesis" 22). In Stephen King's
Pet Sematary, for example, the return of the dead presents us with
the motif of return predicated not only upon a profound mourning
for the death of a loved one – a mourning that never leads to assimilation, interiorization, or idealization, I might add – but also upon
the uncanniness that arises when *what returns* manages to evoke the
unrepresentable, which is what Derrida calls in "Economimesis,"
"the absolute other of the system" (22).

Pet Sematary is the story of Louis Creed, a young physician who
moves from Chicago to a small town in Maine with his wife Rachel,
his two small children, six-year old Ellie and two-year old Gage,
and their cat, Church (short for Churchill). Louis has been hired
to manage the university infirmary. The Creeds are both excited
and anxious about their purchase of a large, colonial-style house

which, even though it is situated on treed land, sits on the side of a highway which is heavily travelled by large trucks. Soon after their arrival, the elderly Jud Crandall, who lives across the road and who befriends Louis Creed, takes them to visit the "Pet Sematary" in the woods behind their house. Jud points out that the cemetery has, for generations, been the burial place for cats and dogs who have been killed on the road. Although the Creeds, including young Ellie, are disturbed by the place, they manage to focus their attentions on the task of settling into their new home. On Louis's first day of work, however, a young student who has been hit by a car dies in Louis's presence but not before rising up to tell Louis, "Don't go beyond, no matter how much you feel you need to, Doctor. The barrier was not meant to be broken" (87). This cryptic utterance takes on meaning for Louis a few days later when his daughter's cat, Church, is killed on the highway and Louis, guided by Jud Crandall, buries the cat in the Micmac burial ground which lies just behind the Pet Sematary. Louis buries the cat according to Jud's instruction and the next day the cat returns, seeming in all respects his former self until Louis notices otherwise:

[Louis] let Church into the house, got his blue dish, and opened a tuna-and-liver cat dinner. As he spooned the gray-brown mess out of the can, Church purred unevenly and rubbed back and forth along Louis's ankles. The feel of the cat caused Louis to break out in gooseflesh, and he had to clench his teeth grimly to keep from kicking him away. His furry sides felt somehow too slick, too thick – in a word, loathsome. (151)

Later, while taking a bath, Louis notices that Church, who has perched on the lowered seat of the toilet and is watching him, is, indeed, *different*:

Church had never looked like this – had never *swayed*, like a snake trying to hypnotize its prey – not before he was fixed and not afterward. For the first time and last time [Louis] played with the idea that this was a different cat, one that just looked like Ellie's ...

It was Church, all right.

"Get out of here," Louis whispered hoarsely at him.

Church stared at him a moment longer – God, his eyes were different, somehow they were different – and then leaped down from the toilet seat. He landed with none of the uncanny grace cats usually display. He staggered awkwardly, haunches thudding against the tub, and then he was gone.

It, Louis thought. *Not he; it.* (152–3)

Like Hawthorne's characters in *The House of the Seven Gables* whose choices consolidate an ancestral debt and contribute to their legacy of guilt, secrets, and misfortune, Louis Creed attempts to repress the horror of what he knows. But the loathing he feels is unmistakable.

When his two-year old son, Gage, is killed on the same road, Louis disinters him after his burial in the town cemetery and then reburies him in the Micmac burial ground. Like the cat, Gage returns from the grave similarly changed and then kills Jud Crandall *and* his own mother. Finally, he is put to (a second) death by his father who then stubbornly returns to the burial ground with the body of his wife, Rachel. The novel ends with Louis Creed sitting alone in his kitchen, playing solitaire. Waiting for Rachel's return, Louis solemnly reflects upon the economy into which he has bought:

What you buy is what you own, and sooner or later what you own will come back to you, Louis Creed thought.

He did not turn around but only looked at his cards as the slow, gritting footsteps approached. He saw the queen of spades. He put his hand on it.

The steps ended directly behind him.

Silence.

A cold hand fell on Louis's shoulder. Rachel's voice was grating, full of dirt.

"*Darling*," it said. (411)

In spite of the horror evoked by King's novel – or maybe because of it – we become aware that the economics of revenance have some basis in disgust. What does it mean "to come back" (from the dead) if, as Louis Creed realizes, "sooner or later what you *own* will come back to you" (emphasis mine)?

In theological accounts of the Crucifixion, it is the hope of salvation that is elaborated in the Resurrection, an event which "filled [Jesus's disciples] with joy" when he "came and stood among them" (John 20:19–20). Indeed, for Christ's death to have redemptive meaning, Christ *must* return from the dead, but such an occasion of return in King's world, as King's novel suggests, inspires not "joy," but rather horror. In other words, whatever returns had better be Christ, or there is going to be trouble.[1]

As far as the story of Christ is concerned, resurrection from the dead implies salvation *from* death – that is, it offers eternal life or presence. King's novel, however, provides a strange countersignature, a twist to an eschatological narrative of infinite being, since it suggests that what returns from the grave is a living-death *nearer* to what Derrida might call "the nonpresence of the other" (*Of Grammatology* 71). The notion that "non-presence" calls attention to the uncanny aspect of what one "owns" or, in any case, "writes," illustrates what Derrida means by the "unrepresentable":

it [like that which utters the word "darling" at the end of King's novel] is unnameable in its singularity. If one could name it or represent it, it would begin to enter into the auto-effective circle of mastery or reappropriation. An economy would be possible. The disgusting X cannot even announce itself as a *sensible* object without being caught up in a teleological hierarchy. It is therefore in-sensible and un-intelligible, irrepresentable and unnameable, the absolute other of the system. ("Economimesis" 22)

If, Derrida renders enigmatic the "eschatological meaning of being as presence" (71) through a "deconstruction of consciousness," (*Of Grammatology* 70) King, draws our attention to the crisis of being which ensues when such deconstruction shows itself not as a redemptive event but rather as a "return" of an unspeakable "non-presence" that abolishes representative distance. King's use of the word "it" to describe the return of Creed's wife from the grave suggests that what returns not only destabilizes the gender categories given by pronominal distinctions, but it also exceeds the ontological determinant, *human*. Indeed, what finally croaks the word "darling" at the end of King's novel is unspeakable in that, in a certain sense, it is *not*.

A BREAK IN THE ECONOMICS OF ESCHATOLOGY

When the dead return in fiction and film they are called by various names: from Nosferatu (meaning the "undead") Dracula, Carmilla, Louis and Lestat, and Church (the cat who returns in Stephen

King's *Pet Sematary*), to the anonymous "things" in George Romero's series of films. As revenants, they walk among the living, either devouring or "infecting" their prey with a condition often ambiguously referred to, at least in vampire lore, as the "dark gift" (a term which has resonance for readers of both vampire fiction *and* deconstruction). Regardless, however, of what the living-dead are "called" – and Stephen King's *Pet Sematary* is again a case in point – their return from the dead is an occasion of horror that reminds us what is at stake in Derrida's remark, in "Plato's Pharmacy," that "writing's case is grave" (103). When Gage, the Creeds' son, comes back, it is, to use the words of one critic, as "a nightmare made real." The nightmare is made real because in spite of Louis Creed's best intentions, Gage's return is out of his father's control. In suggesting a threat to the paternal position, Gage's return from the dead and Louis's loss of control graphically allegorize philosophy's condemnation of writing:

For the written to be the written it must continue to "act" and to be legible even when what is called the author of the writing no longer answers for what he has written, for what he seems to have signed ... This essential drifting due to writing as an iterative structure cut off from all absolute responsibility, from *consciousness* as the authority ... writing orphaned and separated at birth [or, in this case, *death*] from the assistance of its father, is indeed what Plato condemned in the *Phaedrus*. If Plato's gesture is, as I believe, the philosophical movement par excellence, one can measure what is at stake here. ("Signature Event Context" 92)

One can measure what is at stake here because when Gage later kills and then partially devours his mother, Louis is so distraught that, according to Mary Pharr, he "can think of no way to heal her beyond the gruesomely obvious" and returns her body to the Micmac burial ground with equally horrifying results. In the book's epilogue, he waits, both hopeful and despairing, alone in the kitchen until, as Pharr says, "she – it – comes back" (125).

Rachel's return from the dead prompts a return to my previous question: what *does* it mean "to come back" (from the dead) if, as Louis Creed realizes, "sooner or later what you *own* will come back to you"? The phrase "come back to you" has a sinister edge to it. By calling attention to a certain return – of/on "what you [already] own" – the remark implies a return on that which has been sent out, perhaps unconsciously. It returns as something unspeakable because it is unrecognizable as one's own. In "The Roundtable on Translation," Derrida's remarks suggest that writing is like that:

It would be necessary to analyze very closely the experience of hearing someone else read a text you have allegedly written or signed. All of a sudden someone puts a text right in front of you again, in another context, with an intention that is both somewhat yours and not simply yours. Each time it happens, it's a very curious, very troubling experience ... What I can say is that it is never the same text, never an echo, that comes back to you. (158)

King's novel gives us to understand the import of Derrida's remarks, for the return of Rachel Creed draws attention to the uncanniness implicit in the "something" in writing that returns, perhaps through citation, as one's own, even though, as Derrida says in "Roundtable on Translation," "the text's identity has been lost" (158).

In this context, the word "own" is also telling. The most common usage of the transitive verb "to own" is to denote possession. An owner is one who has property. To own also means "to acknowledge authorship, paternity, or possession," all terms indicating rights of property and legitimacy. However, "to own" derives from the Anglo-Saxon *ïgnian*, a word meaning to appropriate, which is synonymous with the verbs to seize, confiscate, usurp, and expropriate. Finally, the word directs our attention to both its Anglo-Saxon and Middle English forms, *unnan* and *unnen*, words which mean "to grant" and thus imply the more benign act of gift-giving. In all cases, the basis of this economy – of "what you buy" and "what you own" – seems to be that of return on an investment, regardless of whether one seizes or grants. However, the essential undecidability of the word produces profound ambivalence around the issue of ownership, inheritance, and legacy. On the one hand, the word suggests that possession comes about by force, while on the other hand, it implies that what one owns has been a gift.

For Derrida, the gift (*le don*) has always been a problem. Derrida contends that a gift cannot be given and remain a gift, for as soon as it is presented it demands restitution and becomes, thus, a debt. That this economy functions in *Pet Sematary* can been seen in one critic's response to the novel when she remarks on the "resurrection" of Church: "It comes home, seemingly a free gift of some god; soon enough, though, the astonished doctor realizes a price has been paid" (Pharr 122). In King's novel, the return of the dead from the grave – "seemingly a free gift of some god" – is anything but "free." Instead, the gift is shown to be an inheritance as well as a debt, the security for which is unspeakable. Although the narrative pivots upon the unspeakable, it brings forward, through the notions of inheritance and indebtedness, the iterability of transgenerational haunting. Since the Creed family – and, especially Louis – is literally consumed by forces which it is not equipped to understand, the narrator draws attention to the legacy of the burial ground, an inheritance which anticipates the arrival of unsuspecting others just as it had awaited the Creeds:

And then the house stood empty in the May sunshine, as it had stood empty on that August day the year before, waiting for the new people to arrive ... as it would wait for other new people to arrive at some future date. A young married couple perhaps, with no children (but with hopes and plans). Bright young marrieds with a taste for Mondavi wine and Löwenbräu beer – he would be in charge of the Northeast Bank's credit department perhaps, she with a dental hygienist's credential or maybe three years' experience as an optometrist's assistant. He would split half a cord of wood for the fireplace, she would wear high-waisted corduroy pants and walk in Mrs. Vinton's field, collecting November's fall grasses for a table centerpiece, her hair in a ponytail, the brightest thing under the gray skies, totally unaware than an invisible Vulture rode the air currents over-head. They would congratulate themselves on their lack of superstition, on their hardheadedness in snaring the house in spite of its history – they would tell their friends that it had been fire-sale priced and joke about the ghost in the attic, and all of them would have another Löwenbräu or another glass of Mondavi, and they would play backgammon or Mille Bourne.
   And perhaps they would have a dog. (396)

A long passage, I include it because it points to the performativity of such an inheritance. That the legacy awaits or even anticipates those who "would congratulate themselves on their lack of super-stition" attests to the vitality of that which continues to live on. It also calls attention to the links between transgenerational haunting, revenance, and indebtedness. In King's novel, the dead return not only because they were not properly buried but also because they represent, in Derridean terms, a certain remainder. That is, as revenants, they return (*as*) the legacy of previous generations in the anticipation of fulfilling a contract which, in *Pet Sematary*, the Creeds will countersign.

King's novel makes this idea abundantly clear in that it demonstrates how the notion of the American dream, founded upon the nostalgia of family life and the right to ownership of land, is predicated upon the violence of colonial appropriation of indigenous lands. In the early pages of the novel, for example, the Creeds are approaching the house they have just purchased – "a big old New England colonial" (16) – beyond which

was a large field for the children to play in, and beyond the field were woods that went on damn near forever. The property abutted state lands, the realtor had explained, and there would be no development in the foreseeable future. The remains of the Micmac Indian tribe had laid claim to nearly eight thousand acres in Ludlow and in the towns east of Ludlow, and the complicated litigation, involving the federal government as well as that of the state, might stretch into the next century. (16)

Prepared to claim it as their own, the Creeds unconsciously take possession of lands that are haunted, if not by "complicated litigation" then certainly by "the *remains* of the Micmac Indian tribe." Although relieved at last to be "home," as the Creeds put it, Louis is also "terrified" for "he had mortgaged twelve years of their lives for this" (16). By the end of the novel, however, when the house becomes less than *heimlich*, the Creeds end up with more (or less) than they bargained for, becoming themselves "collectors of some unpaid symbolic debt," to recall the words of Slavoj Žižek with regards to the return of the dead. Clearly, for the Creeds, the economics of revenance had proven to be viable: "What you buy is what you own," Louis thinks to himself as the hand from the grave reaches out to touch him.

A similar ambivalence is suggested in the use of the word "buy" since it not only means to purchase, but also in its "slang" usage, "to accept, believe, be deceived by, suffer and receive as punishment." Given that the first-person singular of the infinitive *to believe* is *credo* – "I believe" – in Latin, the word *buy*, especially in its slang usage, carries with it an effect of the proper name "Creed" that does not accord with the story of himself that Louis

Creed would *like* to believe. In this sense, the word *buy* functions as Louis Creed's secret name, that is, the name he calls himself in secret through its denial. To the extent that the name Creed draws attention to itself in terms of implying a system of belief, it also evokes the link, again in slang usage, between belief, self-deception and suffering or punishment. Given the many times that Louis Creed justifies his return to the burial ground, he continues, in spite of the warnings he has received, to deceive himself with respect to his intentions. In short, Louis lies to himself. However, in his denial – which is the lie he "owns" – Louis paradoxically tells *to* himself an elaborate fiction of the truth and the truth of his fiction by forgetting. In effect, Louis's relationship *to* himself suggests a system of exchange, an economy in which he – Louis – transfers guilt into a secret account, one which is maintained through "forgetfulness" under the word-name "buy."

For example, while contemplating the reburial of his dead son in the Micmac burial ground – in spite of Jud Crandall's stories regarding both animals and people whose return from the Pet Sematary was an occasion of horror – a vagrant thought crosses Louis's mind: "What do you want to buy next, Louis?" (256). In the novel, this type of inner dialogue is italicized, a technique often used by Stephen King to suggest thought mandated by what Bakhtin would call a "dialogic imperative" (426). King's strategy demonstrates that there can be no actual monologue but, rather, that thought is both heteroglossic and hybridized.[2] In short, the "subject" is a compendium of stratified discourses, not static but always becoming. This instance in the novel is a typical hybridized construction:

For a long time – it seemed like a long time, anyway – [Louis] believed [the knock at the door] was only in his head, a hallucination. But the knocking just went on and on, patient, implacable. And suddenly Louis found himself thinking of the story of the monkey's paw, and a cold terror slipped into him. He seemed to feel it with a total physical reality – it was like a dead hand that had been kept in a refrigerator, a dead hand which had suddenly taken on its own disembodied life and slipped inside his shirt to clutch the flesh over his heart. It was a silly image, fulsome and silly, but oh, it didn't *feel* silly. No.

Louis went to the door on feet he could not feel and lifted the latch with nerveless fingers. And as he swung it open, he thought: *It'll be Pascow* [the student who warned Louis about the barrier before dying in his arms].

Like they said about Jim Morrison, back from the dead and bigger than ever. Pascow standing there in his jogging shorts, big as life and as mouldy as month-old bread. Pascow with his horribly ruined head, Pascow bring the warning again: Don't go up there. What was that old song by the Animals? Baby please don't go, baby PLEASE *don't go, you know I love you so, baby please don't go*

...

[Upon opening the door, Louis finds Jud Crandall standing there.] Time seemed to have turned cleverly back on itself. It was Thanksgiving again. Soon they would put the stiff, unnaturally thickened body of Ellie's cat Winston Churchill into a plastic garbage bag and start off. *Oh, do not ask what is it; let us go and make our visit.* (256–7).

A long passage, it is provocative in that it demonstrates the way that heteroglossia creates what Bakhtin calls "highly particularized *character zones*" (316). As Bakhtin explains,

These zones are formed from the fragments of character speech [*polureč'*], from various forms for *hidden transmission of someone else's word*, from scattered words and sayings belonging *to someone else's speech*, from those invasions into authorial speech of *others'* expressive indicators (ellipsis, questions, exclamations). (316, emphasis mine)

While, to this list, I would add italics and em-dashes, Bakhtin's remarks draw attention to a notion that King's novel demonstrates and that Derrida's writing consistently evokes: that of the subject as multiple and indeterminate, as a discursive textual effect brought about through syntactic markers, pronominal shifts, and citational use of other texts. In short, King's novel functions rather like *Glas* in that it demonstrates how the so-called protagonist is an effect of what Derrida calls citation. Above, "Louis Creed" is an effect of the juxtaposition of texts organized into what Gregory Ulmer might call a collage, the effectiveness of which is that, as Ulmer suggests, "the piece, displaced into a new context, retains associations with its former context" (*Applied Grammatology* 59). In this sense, cultural "texts" such as "The Monkey's Paw," the urban legend of the hand in the refrigerator, the song "Baby Please Don't Go," the cultural icon Jim Morrison, and T.S. Eliot's "The Love Song of J. Alfred Prufrock" not only live on in King's novel through incorporation but are lodged there in what Derrida might call "a host of ghosts." This notion of incorporation is suggested in Bakhtin's remarks which I have italicized in the above passage and which draw attention to one of the concerns addressed in *Pet Sematary*: the writing of a novel as a kind of ventriloquism through which multiple "voices" are, as Derrida might say, "put between quotation marks" or, in other words, encrypted. In this sense, what "returns" in the novel *Pet Sematary* is writing itself, and what "speaks" in the novel are other texts, themselves already inhabited – shall I say, *haunted* – by other texts.

When juxtaposed with Derrida's interest in the crypt-effect of haunting, King's novel demonstrates (in its development of the character of Louis Creed) what enables the practice of cryptomimesis amidst a multiplicity of contradictory texts/voices. In short, Louis Creed has to learn to forget. He has to practise forgetfulness. While kneeling at his son's grave, Louis rationalizes what he is about to do, with the thought, "How could he refuse to take the chance available to him – this one, unbelievable chance – on the basis of [a story of "resurrection" gone bad that Jud had related to him]" (288–9). The caveat that comes to his mind speaks of a dual economy of contradiction and desire:

You're slanting all the evidence in favor of the conclusion you want to produce, his mind protested. *At least tell yourself the goddamned truth about the change in Church* [the cat]. *Even if you want to disqualify the animals ... what about the way he is? Muddled ... that's the best word of all, that sums it up.* (289)

In a way, this passage demonstrates the dynamics of remembering and forgetting, which Nietzsche saw, according to Hayden White, as "the unique attribute of the human animal" (346). To a certain extent, Louis's dilemma suggests that the challenge to being as well as to writing is that of learning to forget, a task which recalls the fantasy of incorporation in that it allows for the unconscious preservation of the "past." In his reading of Nietzsche, White suggests

the extreme case of remembrance of things past would be "the man ... who is condemned to see 'becoming' everywhere." Such a man would – like Roquentin in Sartre's *Nausea* – no longer believe in his own existence, but would instead see everything fly past in an eternal succession and lose himself in the stream of becoming. Without forgetfulness no action is possible, no life is conceivable. (348)

This is the challenge that Louis Creed must face in King's novel in order to act. It is also the challenge facing the reader of Derrida's work. To read "Derrida" is one thing; "to move from reading to criticism," in Barthes's words, is another: "It is no longer to desire the work but to desire one's own language" (qtd. in Kristeva, *Desire* 115). But how can a reader extricate herself from "the work" in order to speak of it when the work invites entanglement, when the work encourages her to "lose [herself] in the stream of becoming," which seems another way of describing citation through which "every sign, linguistic or non-linguistic, spoken or written ... in a small or large unit ... can break with every given context, and engender infinitely new contexts" in a manner which is absolutely illimitable (Derrida, "Signature Event Context" 97). Thus, when Louis Creed thinks, "what you buy is what you own, and sooner or later what you own will come back to you," we are given to understand the potential of this "illimitability" for horror since it not only indicates that there is nothing so haunted as the multiple but also that whatever returns from the "grave" to haunt us must pass through death. Lawrence Schehr's insight into textual production elucidates this notion:

We avoid the ambiguities of the text [if] we choose to believe, *a priori*, that we are dealing with characters ... [This] reduction shows what price we pay for making the facile interconversion from semiosis (or diagesis) to mimesis and back again, as if the two procesess were somehow equivalent. Death is at the center, and we cannot get from one to the other without passing through death. (44)

To pass through death is to effect a transference, however. What gives King's novel its evocative power, and where it exists in a certain correspondence with Derrida's work, is made apparent with its concern with this notion of "crossing."

One way to understand this movement, which is like a transference, is to consider the account by Nicolas Abraham and Maria Torok of how the Wolf Man translated a word – *tieret*, to rub – into an image, that of the floor scrubber who became invested with his desire. What they see is

a genuine dream process in full wakefulness. In order to tell himself his desire [the Wolf Man] has to have recourse to dream distortion. The erogenous fantasy, Grusha the floor scrubber, the washerwoman at the fountain as well as the parents' coitus a tergo, were nothing but a word, translated into an image. The face, the person of the woman are of no importance, provided she illustrates, she embodies the taboo word. (*Wolf Man's* 22)

Here we might even use the word *imago* to suggest what is at stake in crossing the abyss separating the real from the symbolic. Although the term is defined by Jane Gallop as "an unconscious image or cliché"[3] which shapes one's understanding and is predicated upon the workings of transference, we might also understand how the imago's image or cliché could, in fact, be determined by a word or by a fragment of a word, say a sememe, morpheme or phoneme. For example, in King's novel the word "sematary" seems, at first, to be a childish misspelling of the word "cemetery." I find, however, that there is more to the displacement of the "c" to an "s," and of the "e" of cemetery, to an "a," since it suggests a certain passage similar to that proposed by Derrida in the shift from "difference" to *"differance."* In King's novel, the displacement encourages us to think not only in terms of "semantics"; it also leads us to consider the Greek *semantikos* – "significant" – because it draws attention to the Greek *semaino*, which is to signify, evolved from *sema*, sign or tomb. Whereas the displacement suggests a kind of writing to oneself, the return of which is a kind of legacy or an inheritance of that which is a secret, it is towards the *sign* and its relationship to life and death that our attention is directed.

In the novel, "Pet Sematary" is a sign indicating a burial ground for pets. Where the word "pet" leads us to think of the animal who is tamed and treated with fondness, it also allows us to consider the "pet names" of which there are many throughout the novel, "Church" being but one.[4] Similarly, we are also given to think of the familiar or "pet form" of a name – perhaps a translation of the proper name Stephen King since King's first name Stephen, decomposes, in part, into the word "pets." Meanwhile, the proper name Stephen King yields such cryptic anagrams as *kings pet hen* and *king pets hen*, transpositions which turn the proper name into a rebus.[5] This type of encryption of the proper name is mentioned by Derrida in "Roundtable on Translation," when he asks,

Is it possible not to know one's own name? ... Is it possible for the unconscious proper name – that to which the other addresses him/herself

in us, that which responds in us – to be secret? ... Can such a name exist?
– Let us nevertheless put the hypothesis forward. Let's suppose I have a
secret proper name that has nothing to do with my public proper name
or with what anyone may know about me. Suppose also that from time
to time some other may call me by this secret proper name, either by
uttering certain words or syllables or by making certain gestures or signs.
(The secret proper name, the absolute idiom, is not necessarily on the
order of language in the phonic sense but may be on the order of a gesture,
a physical association, a scene of some sort, a taste, a smell. And it is to
this appeal that I would essentially respond, this call that would command
me absolutely.) (106)

As this passage suggests, condensation and displacement work to
produce a name in the same way they produce a rebus-figure in a
dream. I am inclined to think, therefore, that King's novel might
be read as an allegory of cryptomimesis, since it reflects a debate
of the author *with himself* with regards to the link between writing
and (living-)death and the decomposition of the proper name. The
dialogue is about a particular economy – an uncanny contract
predicated upon burial, revenance, and haunting – which can again
be thought through the crypt.

  "Writing's case is grave" (says Derrida in "Plato's Pharmacy")
and through this assertion we understand why Derrida says of the
crypt that it is "perhaps itself the contract with the dead" (*"Fors"*
xxxviii). To consider this "contract" we will examine the word *case*
because it calls attention (1) to the instance of a thing's occurring;
(2) to writing as a "case history" as in the record of a person's
ancestry, psychoanalytic record, or medical history of disease; (3)
to what encloses something in a box; (4) to law as settled by
decided case, and (5) to the grammatical term to identify a pronoun. "Case" derives from the Latin *casus*, fall, which in French
is *tomber*, and its cognate *capsa* (*copere* hold). Why then is the case
of writing grave?

  Derrida *makes a case* for writing when he takes issue with
Heidegger over the issue of "essence." He does so by suggesting
that both essence and the so-called subject are an effect of language.
When Heidegger, in his essay, "The Thing," makes a case for an
a priori necessity of essence, Derrida argues in *"Fors"* that the
"Thing" is necessarily a "crypt effect" (xiii), not because it is
predicated upon the notion of language as the "house" of being in

which man "dwells" – these metaphors evoke a particular nostalgia for "home" – but rather upon the understanding of language as being motivated by and/or performative of its *ties* with the dead as well as being performative of the "subject" as a spectral effect (of the text and thus of writing). When Derrida uses the phrase "what is engaged and bound" to describe the crypt effect (of writing), he makes explicit the contractual aspects of language in terms of indebtedness, inheritance, promise, pledge, and betrothal, all of which imply the spirit of return in that which is yet to come, a phenomenon which Derrida calls elsewhere a "hauntology":

Repetition *and* first time: this is perhaps the question of the event as question of the ghost. *What is* a ghost? What is the *effectivity* or the *presence* of a specter, that is, of what seems to remain as ineffective, virtual, insubstantial as a simulacrum? Is there *there*, between the thing itself and its simulacrum, an opposition that holds up? Repetition *and* first time, but also repetition *and* last time, since the singularity of any *first time* makes of it also a *last time*. Each time it is the event itself, a first time is a last time. Altogether other. Staging for the end of history. Let us call it a *hauntology*. This logic of haunting would not be merely larger and more powerful than an ontology or a thinking of Being (of the "to be," assuming that it is a matter of Being in the "to be or not to be," but nothing is less certain). It would harbor within itself, but like circumscribed places or particular [crypt] effects, eschatology and teleology themselves. It would *comprehend* them, but incomprehensibly. (*Specters* 10)

In a word, "hauntology" calls attention to both Derrida's kinship with the Gothic in terms of its structuring principle, as well as his concern to demonstrate the performativity of the crypt in terms of its staging ontology and eschatology as phantom effects.

THE LOGIC OF HAUNTING

When Derrida says, in "*Fors*," "the crypt keeps an undiscoverable place, with reason," (xii) it is the logic of haunting that becomes evident. This logic of haunting is what produces "the Thing" as a kind of contractual effect predicated upon "what is engaged and bound" ("*Fors*" xiii) transgenerationally. Although this contract takes place in secret, it is not only unconscious but also active. In

Specters of Marx, Derrida alludes to this spectral effect when he says that

among all the temptations I will have to resist ... there would be the temp-
tation of memory: to recount what was for me, and for those of my *generation* who shared it during a whole lifetime, the experience of Marxism,
the quasi-paternal figure of Marx, the way it fought in us with other fili-
ations, the reading of texts and the interpretation of a world in which the
Marxist inheritance was – and still remains, and so it will remain – absolutely and thoroughly determinate. One need not be a Marxist or a communist in order to accept this obvious fact. We all live in a world, some
would say a culture, that still bears, at an incalculable depth, the mark of
this inheritance whether in a directly visible fashion or not. (13–14)

What Derrida is describing here is the condition of haunting in
terms of a "world" or a "culture" that "bears" the dead: *bears* in
the sense of "giving birth to" and also of conveyance, sustainment,
and transport. This notion of an active contractual relationship
with the dead is similarly referred to by Michel de Certeau when
he asserts that "discourse about the past has the status of being
the discourse of the dead. The object circulating in it is only the
absent, while its meaning is to be a language shared ... by living
beings. Whatever is expressed engages a group's communication
with itself through this reference to an absent, third party that
constitutes its past. The dead are the objective figure of an *exchange*
among the living" (qtd. in Schor 3, emphasis mine). What is telling
in de Certeau's remarks is the evocation of haunting and mourning
in terms which suggest that our relationship to the dead is an
economic one. Esther Schor develops this notion in her discussion
of mourning within the social and textual practice of the British
Enlightenment, asserting that

the Enlightenment culture of mourning was instrumental in mediating
between received ideas of virtue, both classical and Christian, and a
burgeoning, property-based commercial society. In the first chapter of his
Theory of Moral Sentiments, Adam Smith designates an originary act of
sympathy for the dead as the motivation for all subsequent occasions of
sympathy. The most urgent significance of this myth lies in Smith's *economic* metaphors for the relations between the living and the dead.

According to Smith, sympathetic "tribute" "paid" to the dead is not given freely; rather it is an "indebted" consideration for the moral value with which the dead endow the living. Moreover, the diffusion of sympathy from the grave outward is characterized as a series of exchanges; sympathy is extended to the mourner by a disinterested party in exchange for a curbing of grief. (5)

Schor's remarks suggest the extent to which the logic of haunting is predicated upon the economics of revenance. The "incalculable depth" of this economy cannot be underestimated since it functions, cryptically, to produce the experience of interiority and exteriority as crypt effects of language returning to itself as the subject. This system of exchange is suggested by Derrida's remark that "the cryptophore engages itself toward the dead, grants the dead, as collateral, a *mortgage* within itself, a pledge within the body" ("*Fors*" xxxviii, emphasis mine).

Stephen King's novel illuminates the terms of the psychic economy to which Derrida refers. In *Pet Sematary*, the Creeds have indeed made such a "pledge" by taking out a mortgage. But a mortgage requires collateral: that which is handed over as security for fulfillment of a contract or payment of a debt, and is liable to forfeiture in case of failure to pay. This notion seems evident in Stephen King's naming the son Gage, since it is the son who is a *mort/gage*, literally, a "dead pledge" that, paradoxically, returns from the grave to fulfill a contract. A pledge, moreover, is also a promise and the novel does concern itself with the uncanniness of what, like a ghost, always promises (to return): in particular, *writing*. The link between text and mortgage is uncanny, which is what E.M. Forster means, in *Aspects of the Novel*, when he says, "Once in the realm of the fictitious, what difference is there between an apparition and a mortgage" (103)? Although it is not made explicit in King's text, what returns (to oneself) would amount to an inheritance – a legacy – it would live on even beyond the grave from which it continues to state its case.

In a *fort/da* economy such as this, one's ghost – what remains (of writing) after one's death – might be what lives on. The economy of writing that Derrida calls "expropriation – the attempt to bring back one's ghostly inheritance" – is strangely reminiscent of the economy that King's novel proposes and materializes. Consider

Derrida's remarks in "The Roundtable on Translation," where he is discussing his response to hearing himself quoted by another:

This is what goes on with texts. When I saw, for example, that it was a piece of "Living On" that Donato was quoting, I was reading it through Donato's text: it was something very strange which returned utterly without me. I thought: That's not bad, but it's not the same. It's never the same in *any* case, and it never returns. This is both a bad thing and a good thing. Obviously, if it came back, that would also be terrible. One wants it to return exactly like it is, but then one also knows very well that if it did come back exactly like it is, one would have only one wish and that is to run away. (158–9)

Although familiar, it is never the same in *any* case, and because of that *it* never returns except as difference. Derrida's remarks about writing intersect with King's novel at the point of no return. Both posit that a return, in Derrida's words, "would ... be terrible" since – and I think the horror genre bears this out – "if it did come back exactly like it is, one would have only one wish and that is to run away." For Derrida, the return of the same, although impossible, would be terrible, for it would herald a movement so uncanny as to be unbearable. As it is, what does return is undeniably uncanny anyway. The point at which Derrida and King intersect – and which the Gothic has consistently turned upon – can be heard in Derrida's remark on hearing his text cited, in that nevertheless, "it [like Rachel Creed?] was *something very strange* which returned *utterly without me.*"

"WE HAVE PUT HER LIVING IN THE TOMB": AN AESTHETICS OF REVENANCE

Since it appears to harbour a contradiction, let us momentarily dwell upon Derrida's use of the word "without," for it acts as a cryptic marker directing our attention to an aspect of cryptomimesis that I would like to call the uncanny aesthetics of revenance. Let us first recall the anguished cries of Poe's Roderick Usher, with which I opened this work: "*We have put her living in the tomb!* ... I ... tell you that I heard her first feeble movements in the hollow coffin. I heard them – many, many days ago ...! *I tell you that she now stands* without *the door.*" While the word *without* denotes an absence or a lack (of a door?), it also functions as a spatial determinant indicating where "she" – Madeline Usher – stands (having returned from the crypt and, thereby, resisting untimely burial). We understand that a barrier – namely, a door – exists *necessarily* between Roderick Usher and his sister, Madeline, for when the doors are finally breached, and Madeline Usher crosses the threshold, Roderick joins his sister in death:

As if in the superhuman energy of his utterance there had been found the potency of a spell – the huge antique panels to which the speaker pointed, threw slowly back, upon the instant, their ponderous and ebony jaws. It was the work of the rushing gust – but then without those doors there *did* stand the lofty and enshrouded figure of the lady Madeline of Usher. There was blood upon her white robes, and the evidence of some bitter struggle upon every portion of her emaciated frame. For a moment she remained, trembling and reeling to and fro upon the threshold – then, with a low moaning cry, fell heavily inward upon the person of her brother, and in her horrible and now final death-agonies bore him to the floor a corpse, and a victim to the terrors he had dreaded. (547)

Having burst from the copper-lined vault, Madeline Usher is a living-dead who returns to settle a certain account with her twin: a debt upon which we can only speculate since it remains to be seen. What has happened?

   Abraham and Torok's analysis of the Wolf Man suggests a curious parallel between Madeline Usher's interment by her twin brother and the fantasy of incorporation. In fact, Abraham and Torok's remarks regarding the Wolf Man's "incorporation" of his sister seem indebted to Poe's story of the ill-fated twins in terms of "speaking" the Wolf Man's unconscious: "such an incorporation of the sister is ... understood as the only possible means of combining within her two incompatible roles: that of Ego Ideal and that of Love Object. It was the only means of loving her in order not to annihilate her, and of annihilating her in order not to love her" (*Wolf Man's* 4). When his wife ended her life, the Wolf Man ultimately suffered what Abraham and Torok refer to as an attack of "depressive agitation worse than any he had ever experienced" (7), a diagnosis which seems to accord with Roderick Usher's agitation following his sister's interment. According to Abraham and Torok, it was such an illness – an "identification with the mourning of the internal Father" (7) *for* the sister as a love object – that protected the Wolf Man from the "grave danger" of "making a link between his erotic desire for his sister and her suicide" (7). Although in Poe's story Madeline Usher does not commit suicide, the account of her entombment and her return from the vault draw attention to the "grave dangers" that the fantasy of incorporation implies and that cryptomimesis draws upon to give "voice" to what Derrida calls the "living feminine," of which he tellingly remarks "one buries or burns what is *already dead* so that life, the living feminine, will be reborn and regenerated from these ashes" ("Oto-biographies" 26).

If we recall that the function of a crypt is, in Derrida's words, "to save [a] living death" through preservation, we can read the correspondence between the fantasy of incorporation – which cryptomimesis mimes – and Poe's story, "The Fall of the House of Usher," which cryptomimesis incorporates. What is central to this claim is the notion that the repression with which each (cryptomimesis *and* incorporation) is concerned "is not confined to images, thoughts, and fantasies but above all acts on words themselves" (Rand, *The Shell* 18). In the case of the Wolf Man, for example, it is the word *tieret* that functions, albeit not exclusively, as the magic word that, says Gregory Ulmer, "carries with it the effect of a proper name" (*Applied Grammatology* 62). Ulmer points out that for the Wolf Man, "other words – *goulfik*, (the fly of his father's trousers) and *vidietz* (a witness, alluding to the glimpse of the primal scene) – are also part of the name. The name is magic because it has only to be uttered for the bearer to obtain 'actual or sublimated sexual satisfaction' (the name as symptom)" (62). To understand what is at stake in the Wolf Man's cryptonymy is to illuminate the mechanism of cryptomimesis. Ulmer has argued that the Wolf Man's cryptonymy

did not operate by the usual procedures of representation – the symbolizing or hiding of one word behind another, or one thing by a word or a word by a thing. Rather, [the Wolf Man's] names were generated by picking out from the extended series of "allosemes" – the catalogue of uses available for a given word – a particular usage, which is then translated into a synonym (creating thus even greater distance from the secret name). The path from crypt to speech may follow either semantic or phonic paths, with the play between homonyms and synonyms being part of the mechanism. Thus, the allosemes of *Tieret*, for example to rub, to grind, to wound, to polish – provide a range of associations and dissociations among the semantic fields related to rubbing and/or wounding-scrubbing that provide the Wolf Man with his vocabulary. (62–3)

Derrida's remarks on the Wolf Man's *Verbarium* confirm that the linking of the uttered word to the secret name is a labyrinth comprised of "non-semantic associations, purely phonetic combinations":

The Wolf Man's Magic Word shows how a sign, having become arbitrary, can remotivate itself. And into what labyrinth, what multiplicity of heterogeneous places, one must enter in order to track down the cryptic motivation, for example in the case of *TR*, when it is marked by a proper-name effect (here, *tieret*), and when, consequently, it no longer belongs simply to the internal system of language. Such motivation does nevertheless function within the system and no linguistic consciousness can deny it. For example, when *Turok* (Turk, the Turkish flag in the dream of the moon with a star) says (?), means (?), translates (?), points out (?), represents (?), or *in any case* also imitates, induces the word-thing *tieret*. ("*Fors*" xlvii)

That Derrida has taken on the task of laying down such a motivated labyrinth is remarked by Ulmer who points out that "the TR of the *Verbarium* accounts for the GL of *Glas*" (*Applied Grammatology* 63). This observation draws our attention to a writing practice predicated upon the break-up of words and the decomposition of the proper name which Ulmer suggests is "the key to the production of the text" (63). Ulmer also discusses Derrida's notion of the proper name as the "permeable membrane, (the tympan, the hymen, allowing contamination between the inside and outside)" (63).

The notion linking the hymen (and the tympan) to the proper name is central to understanding the correspondence, in terms of cryptomimesis, between Poe's work and Derrida's. Firstly, Poe's proper name gets *countersigned* as a matter of course in Derrida's work, the countersignature appearing consistently through Derrida's evocation of the uncanny intersections between architecture and mourning, and between the family and the tomb. Similarly, "*Fors*" "Cartouches" and *Glas* are concerned with the complications of ghostly returns and *unheimlich* conditions, concerns that are also suggested by Mark Wigley who argues that the "ongoing subtext" of *Glas* is "the *oikos* as tomb" (174). This observation just as well describes "The Fall of the House of Usher" in which the figures of the house and the family are in conjunction with the tomb as their (living-dead) centre. Even though the "subjects" of *Glas* are Hegel and Genet, in a certain way, Poe's "work" is heard as a kind of "refrain-effect" in Derrida's.[6] It manifests in a way that recalls the doublings in Poe's text where the distinctions slip between the interior of the Usher house and its exterior, while Roderick Usher's ballad, "The Haunted Palace" reproduces the events which end in the collapse of the house and the death of the ill-fated twins.

What haunts Derrida's work is the figure of the (fissured) house, at the heart of which is a crypt, the inhabitant of which is the harbinger of the uncanny. As Mark Wigley points out, "a rhetoric of the house can be found throughout Derrida's texts" (106). Resonating as a kind of subtext, the rhetoric of the house demonstrates not only that "the house's ability to domesticate is its capacity to define inside and outside" (107) but also that the "structural slippage from *heimliche* to *unheimliche* [comes about because] that which supposedly lies outside the familiar comfort of the home turns out to be inhabiting it all along, surfacing only [as in the case of Madeline Usher] in a return of the repressed as a foreign element that strangely seems to belong in the very domain that renders it foreign" (108). Derrida's work is indeed "rendered strange" and not only because it resonates with his rereadings of Freud's essay "The Uncanny"; it also draws upon what has been inhabiting it all along as a foreign element: the crypt effect of Poe's name, among others. To this end, the name Poe appears to have been "decomposed" in Derrida's work into *peau*, skin, hide, peel, also *avoir dans la peau* – to be head over heels in love; *faire peau neuve*, to cast its skin, turn over a new leaf. What is it about Derrida and Peau?

Here is one place where hidden in Poe is Derrida's *hide*, where he *saves* his own skin, so to speak: "If I write two texts at once, *you will not be able to castrate me*" (*Speech and Phenomena* 81, emphasis mine). In *Glas* there is a peephole and through it both Genet's tattoos and the parchment of the Torah are seen to have something in common:

Our-Lady-of-the-Flowers ... will have prescribed the *glas* form: "The great nocturnal occupation, admirably suited for enchanting the darkness, is tattooing. Thousands and thousand of little jabs [*coups*] with a fine needle prick the skin and draw blood, and figures that you would read as most extravagant are flaunted in the most unexpected places. When the rabbi slowly unrolls the Torah, a mystery sends a shudder through the whole epidermis, as when one see a colonist undressing. The grimacing of all that blue on white skin. (240)

And we might even say that the tissue in question – as well as what remains of the proper name Poe – is also that which lies *between* Derrida and Poe, a permeable membrane allowing contamination between an inside and an outside – in Derrida's terms, a hymen.

In *Applied Grammatology*, Gregory Ulmer claims that Derrida finds Ponge's signature especially instructive, since Ponge takes the side of the proper in order, like Genet, to appropriate objects (116). Ulmer points out that, "what disgusts Ponge [according to Derrida] is not 'the dirty' but 'the soiled,' the proper which has been affected, which usually happens (in his poems) 'by liquid means' (the liquid 'L' of *Glas*) which must be absorbed or sponged up with linen or tissue, termed a 'mass of *ignoble* tissues'" (*Applied Grammatology* 115–16). Thus, Poe/peau: tissue from OF *tissu*, rich material: connective, muscular, nervous, adipose, mass of cells, interwoven series, set, collection. Given that "the signature of the proper name can also play the role of a cache (sheath or fleece) to conceal another signature" (*Applied Grammatology* 132) it is, as Ulmer suggests, "never finally possible to decide who or what signs" (132). Taken in this context, Peggy Kamuf's remark – "the hymen is between – them" (xxxvix) – tells of the undecidability that enfolds one in the other – Derrida/Poe – in certain quasi-architectural scenes as well as the sense of how the *images* of a text are predicated upon the dissemination of the proper name:

The phrase retains both of the word's most common senses, that is the hymen as both the veil-like tissue across the vagina that remains intact as long as virginity does, and, in a somewhat archaic but still comprehensible sense (in English as well as French), hymen as the union or marriage which is consummated by the act that ruptures it (i.e., the hymen in the first sense). In other words, it is between them, that is, it divides them, marks their difference as a sexual difference of inside from outside; and it is between them, that is, it joins them or unites them in a symbolic union. ... The partition of the hymen partitions itself, departs from itself and from any proper meaning. It does so by articulating the two senses of articulation: dividing-joining, by enfolding the one in the other undecidably. Is not, therefore, the hymen a more general name for all these jealous partitionings? (xxxvix)

Here the word *hymen* draws attention to itself as a partitioning device that, like the crypt, is a *simulacrum* producing the effect of an interior – say that of a text – that is accessible only through a certain kind of violence that has *already* produced the possibility of an interior in the first place. Its implications for reading as well as writing can be found in Heidegger's remarks about reading Kant: "Certainly, in order to wring from what the words say, what it is that they want to say, every interpretation must necessarily use violence" (Kant 138). In a similar vein, Heidegger also asserts in *An Introduction to Metaphysics*, "the actual interpretation must show what does not stand in the words and is nevertheless said. To accomplish this the exegete must use violence" (162). Derrida, like Heidegger, understands the notion that violence is necessary in terms of reading (and writing [the crypt]). Let's call such reading crypt-analysis, since, as Derrida says, it requires procedures that are far from those of classical psychoanalysis, which relies on a form of hermeneutics *vis-à-vis* the metaphor of the unconscious. In crypt-analysis, the "crypt" could not be read either literally or as a metaphor because it is the condition of reading, itself. In these terms, crypt-analysis avoids turning a text into a catalogue of hieroglyphics in which one system of symbols is merely converted to another. Rather than being restorative, crypt-analysis is productive, which is why Derrida insists that the crypt is always already "*built* by violence" ("*Fors*" xv):

To track down the path to the tomb, then to violate a sepulcher: this is what the analysis of a cryptic incorporation is like. The idea of violation [*viol*] might imply some kind of transgression of a right, the forced entry of a penetrating, digging, force, but the violated sepulcher *itself* was never "legal." It is the very tombstone of the illicit, and marks the spot of an extreme pleasure [*jouissance*], a pleasure entirely *real* though walled up, buried alive in its own prohibition. ("*Fors*" xxxiv)

The idea of violation is at the heart of the House of Usher. At the heart of that house also lies a hollow tomb that in silence demonstrates what is at stake in Derrida's remarks. For a number of reasons, the crypt in question evokes the fantasy of incorporation rather than introjection, not the least of which is that it holds a living-dead. It has also been "built by violence." We are told that in "remote feudal times" it had been used "for the worst purposes of a donjon-keep," (Poe 542) a judicial structure that Foucault might well describe as an "architectural apparatus" ("Panopticism" 201) that *produces* the prisoner (or subject, for that matter) as an effect of the mechanisms of disciplinary power.

Because the crypt was used previously as a dungeon, we are alerted to the fact that those who were held prisoner were thus subject to certain punitive mechanisms exerted on the body. The narrator's mention that the family vault had also been used as "a place of deposit for powder, or other highly combustible substance" (542) suggests how (the fantasy of) the crypt functions to house or to lodge certain *volatile* materials that, in the realm of desire might be maintained while under interdiction. Thus, to recall Derrida's remarks above, we can appreciate how the crypt functions to keep safe "an extreme pleasure [*jouissance*], a pleasure entirely *real* though walled up, buried alive [like Madeline Usher] in its own prohibition" ("*Fors*" xxxiv). Poe's story reminds us that what is "buried alive" must indeed be illicit for even though Roderick Usher *knows* that his sister has been entombed – he has heard for "many minutes, many hours, many days" her "feeble movements in the hollow coffin" – he says, "I *dared* not speak!" (547). Presumably, Usher's reticence to act upon the knowledge of his sister's live burial is due to his horror at a mistake. However, a closer look at his own ballad of "The Haunted Palace" suggests that there is more at stake than a terrible error in judgment. And while we discover how the illicit finds its way into Poe's story, we understand its entry into Derrida's writing through similar means of entombment.

PERISTALSIS: A LOVE STORY

It is important to recall that the ballad – described by the narrator as a "rhymed verbal improvisation" (539) – was *written* by Roderick Usher who recites it while playing a guitar. If we recall that the events in "The Haunted Palace" reproduce and foretell the events which end in the collapse of the house of Usher, and the deaths of

Roderick and Madeline, we realize that the ballad gives us access to a corridor of inquiry not previously accessible in our consideration of the spatial determinants of the rhetoric of the house. Namely, the rhythmic or semiotic components of language, which are reduced to the function of "naming-predicating" in the prose, are re-activated in the ballad, thus bringing us into proximity with the affective forces that are subordinated in the symbolic.

In a work published posthumously, Nicolas Abraham suggests that the study of rhythm in Poe's "The Raven," reveals "certain aspects of the poem's general affective movement" (*Rhythms* 126). (This "affective movement" appears analogous to what Kristeva calls semiotic activity in poetic language.) In Usher's ballad, rather than in the story, we become aware of the difference between the narrated event and the "affective movements" or rhythmic instances:

> In the greenest of our valleys
> By good angels tenanted
> Once a fair and stately palace –
> Snow-White Palace – reared its head.
> In the monarch Thought's dominion –
> It stood there!
> Never seraph spread his pinion
> Over fabric half so fair! (539)

In this first stanza, for example, the beat is thrown off slightly in the fourth line with the phrase "Snow-White Palace" and, likewise, by the repetition of the word "palace" which seems, at first, to function as internal rhyme but instead sets up a note of discord, especially when the palace, which is personified, recalls the uncanniness of Usher's house with its "vacant eye-like windows" (532). One effect of this discord is to jolt us out of the kind of reverie that *the narrator has fallen into*, in which he finds it difficult to distinguish waking from dreaming. But there is more to it than that.

Although we are drawn back into a familiar rhythm in the next line – "In the monarch Thought's dominion" – we are jolted once again – only harder this time – by the emphatic, "It stood there!" Like Poe's poem, "The Raven," the ballad of the haunted palace seems, at first, to induce drowsiness, and the rhythm to promise, as Abraham notes of the other poem, "that this gentle rocking will land us safe and sound" (*Rhythms* 126). But there is nothing safe and sound in store. The ballad instead dramatizes a double bind. It encourages our attempts to fall into reverie and it demands that we awaken with a start. What is the thing that awakens? In their analysis of the Wolf Man's nightmare of the wolves, Abraham and Torok point out that it is the Wolf Man's "crying out" in fear of being eaten that awakens him. They ask, "how can he sleep with a 'cry' inside?" (*Wolf Man's* 40). Do they mean a cry/pt? These and Abraham's comments on "The Raven" suggest a certain relationship between the rhythmic effects of that poem and the "The Haunted Palace," drawing attention to the correspondence between Poe's story and the fantasy of incorporation:

The discord between meaning and rhythm is precisely what is so eminently exemplary. Of what? Of the fact that the reality breaking in upon the dream is not an external event but a harrowing wish whose specter reaches consciousness in the form of hallucinatory representations. The exemplary creation ... resides in the fact that one and the same rhythm underlies both the abrupt rise of anxiety and the increasingly tense refusal to submit to it. In the story [of "The Raven"], an attempt is made to reassure oneself; in the rhythm, mounting anxiety. All the rhythm says is: a troubling obstacle is unsettling sleep. (*Rhythms* 127)

Interruptions in the rhythm of the ballad strongly suggest the presence of a "troubling obstacle" that, like the Wolf Man's crying out, is "unsettling sleep." While the ballad draws attention to the way that troubling obstacles manifest themselves arrhythmically, it also suggests that attempts to repress the discord come about in the form of a "harrowing wish" to "reassure oneself." This affective movement mimes the fantasy of incorporation. By identifying this movement as "peristalsis," Abraham draws attention to the digestive link between incorporation and the refusal to mourn. According to Abraham, the rhythm of incorporation is analogous to peristaltic movement: "a maximum opening at first, then its repetition, and, once the prey is ingested, a gradual contraction to push it further inward, then, finally a definitive closure" (128). This notion also suggests what is implied in Derrida's concern with the "reading effect" of his writing which Mark Wigley has observed is "identified with the spacing of rhythm" (175). While Poe's ballad draws attention to the peristaltic action at work in the house of Usher, it can also shed light on how Derrida's concern with the relationship between writing and the fantasy of incorporation is laid out in terms of *indigestion* and *vomiting* (to the inside).

In Poe's ballad, disturbances in rhythm enact the entombment of the "old-time," an incorporative act which gives rise to the spectral return of "Vast forms that move fantastically/*To a discordant melody*" (540). In Derrida's case, "the discordant melody" also takes peristaltic form:

> When I say that *Glas* is also working on the "reading effect," what I mean in particular is that it has as one of its principle themes reception (assimilation, digestion, absorption, introjection, *incorporation*) or non-reception (exclusion, foreclosure, rejection and once again, but this time as internal expulsion, *incorporation*), thus the theme of internal or external vomiting, of mourning-work and everything that gets around to or comes to *throwing up*. But *Glas* does not only treat these themes; in a certain way, it offers itself up to all these operations. (qtd. in Wigley 174)

So, a text like *Glas* not only takes incorporation as its theme but it also does what it says: it performs the fantasy of incorporation that Poe's story also accomplishes. To a certain extent, the intersection of the two – Poe and Derrida – might be thought of as "The Fall of the *Glas* House of Usher." Such a title would draw attention to the structuring principle of incorporation that, producing *an architecture of mourning*, structures not only the text but also the subject. The question that Derrida poses in "*Fors*" suggests what is significant about a writing that has an architectural "relation" to a crypt and is, moreover, cryptically motivated:

> What is called Thinking? [saying that] ... the Thing is to be thought out *starting from* the Crypt, the Thing as a "crypt effect" ... It is a kind of "false unconscious," an "artificial" unconscious lodged like a prosthesis, a graft in the heart of an organ, within the *divided self*. A very specific and peculiar place, highly circumscribed, to which access can nevertheless only be gained by following the routes of a different topography. ("*Fors*" xiii)

In this passage we can see Derrida's debt not only to Abraham and Torok but also to Poe in that cryptomimesis mimes the undecidability of the structuring process of the "The Fall of the House of Usher." Poe, like Derrida, is concerned with "tracing" a certain cryptic "architecture" of mourning. With Poe's text, as with Derrida's, we feel that what is at work is a kind of framing device, the net effect of which is the production of an uncanny space, or what might be called an artificial unconscious. Such an uncanny space evokes the fantasy of incorporation in which the crypt "always *marks* an effect of impossible or refused mourning (melancholy *or* morning)" ("*Fors*" xxi, emphasis mine). For Derrida, this "marking" amounts to writing *on* "The Fall of the House of Usher." In general, such a writing amounts to disruptions in the organization and maintenance of interior space which take place through the violence of exclusion and repression. It also draws upon whatever threatens the borders of that space.

In Poe's story, shifting movements of framing and referentiality – including the con/fusion between the Usher *family* and the (proper name of the) family mansion – contribute to a kind of disturbance of what Derrida would call "the 'normal' system of reference" ("Before the Law" 213), that is, traditional mimesis with its values and assumptions of realism. "The Fall of the House of Usher" folds in on itself, allegorizing its own process of encryption/incorporation and, like Derrida's work, offers itself as the uncanny model of its own making. But in Poe's text, as in Derrida's writing, allegory is not used in the traditional sense of allegoresis, which Gregory Ulmer describes as "adhering to the model of the hieroglyph in which the particular object of nature or daily life is taken over as a conventional sign for an idea" ("Object of Post-Criticism" 97). Rather, Poe's text models the allegorical impetus of cryptomimesis: it demonstrates that allegory is "not an arbitrary representation of the idea which it [portrays]. It [is] instead the concrete expression of that idea's material foundation" (Buck-Morss 56). This is a notion which Derrida has clearly taken to heart when he remarks in "*Fors*," "What is a crypt? What if I were writing on one now?" (xi). I could say the same.

The Question of the Tomb

As allegory, Poe's work plays upon the divisions which make the *text*, like the House of Usher – the name and the structure – a "very specific and peculiar place, highly circumscribed" (to recall Derrida's remarks). In a certain sense, "The Fall of the House of Usher" – including the house, the crypt, the patronym, and the story – acts as synecdoche for Derrida's writing practice, anticipating his concern with the implicit violence of architecture. This notion is voiced by Mark Wigley who points out that, for Derrida, the house is

the very principle of violence. To dominate is always to house, to place in the *domus*. Domination is domestication [of the feminine].

Yet the house does not simply precede what it domesticates. The house is itself an effect of suppression. The classical figure of the feminine is that which lacks its own secure boundaries, producing insecurities by disrupting boundaries, and which therefore must be housed by masculine force that is no more than the ability to maintain rigid limits, or, more precisely, the effect of such limits, the representation of a space, a representation that is not only violently enforced by a range of disciplinary structures (legal, philosophical, economic, aesthetic, technical, social, and so on), but is itself a form of violence. Masculinity is not only erection but also enclosure, the logic of the house is as phallocentric as that of the tower. (137–8)

Here we realize how Poe's text is its own example of domestic violence. We also realize how a return from the crypt – as implied by the figure of Madeline Usher – occasions a threat to the "secure boundaries" and "rigid limits" maintained by the "logic of the house." It is in this sense that Poe's work, to use Derrida's phrase, "can *play the law*" in that it has

a power to produce performatively the statements of the law, of the law that literature can be, and not just of the law to which literature submits. Thus literature itself makes law, emerging in that place where the law is made. Therefore, under certain determined conditions, it can exercise the legislative power of linguistic performativity to sidestep existing law from which, however, it derives protection and receives its conditions of emergence. ("Before the Law" 216)

It is in this relation to the law that cryptomimesis is tacitly indebted to Poe who, as Joseph Riddel points out, is "evoked [throughout the "Envois,"] as a metonymic figure for a certain notion of 'literature'" (19). Riddell also claims that it is Poe's work that underscores Derrida's concern for the relation of "literature" to philosophy in that for Derrida, it is important to

consider the already deformed dialogue between psychoanalysis (or philosophy) and literature, from the margin of an "America" and a kind of "literature" that is neither philosophy nor literature. It is Poe, his texts, his crypt, that at once resist and motivate the analytical performance, reading and writing, because they will not themselves be read, mastered, by the methodology they seem to exemplify. For as Derrida says, what kind of science or reflexive clarity is obtained when the literary example provides a clearer scene of analysis, of reading itself, than the science that has to deform it or misread it into a perfect case of method, a method that is complete and total in mastering what it reads, its own example. (19)

Although Riddel goes on to "deform" Poe's story (as I myself enjoy doing), his remarks draw attention to the double play that exists between "The Fall of the House of Usher" and cryptomimesis: "The 'House of Usher' is built out of old books, the fragments of legends, romances, superstitions, and quasi-scientific metaphors, all erected upon a 'hollow coffin' that must be protected even as it is ultimately opened and revealed as the place of just another missing body, another simulacrum of a simulacrum" (135).

It is telling that Riddel refers to the "hollow coffin" of Poe's story and only indirectly to Madeline Usher, whose return from the crypt signals the collapse of her brother Roderick, the man whom Riddel describes as "that fictional figure of the imminent apocalypse waiting within every genealogical fiction of descent or ascent" (116).

It is also telling that in his lengthy remarks regarding Poe's story, Riddel omits any discussion of Madeline Usher except to mention that Roderick's "dispatching of his sister to the tomb, is a last futile gesture to maintain the structure of 'house' and 'family,' a last will to signification, a final attempt to preserve presence or life by a reinstallation of some sign of presence there where the center is absented" (134). Although Riddel concedes that in Poe, the dead woman is the "figure of the text," his failure to make any real mention of Madeline Usher (not even her name!) suggests that an economy of exclusion similar to the one he ascribes to Roderick Usher is at stake and that his omission recapitulates the principles of violence of the house with which Derrida is concerned.

One wonders what it is that Riddel desires to maintain if not the violent representation of a certain space that excludes the feminine, especially if, as Wigley mentions, the "feminine" is that "which lacks its own secure boundaries, producing insecurities by disrupting boundaries." By focusing his attention exclusively on Roderick Usher and the narrator, Riddel accomplishes the anxious deferral that he ascribes to them in their reading of "Mad Trist." This reading, says Riddel, "is employed by the narrator to defer both his and Usher's sense of the torment, the question, encrypted at the center of the house. Yet, it can only amplify the question of the tomb" (134) as it is posed by Madeline Usher.

At this point, I should note that I am focusing on Riddel's remarks because they "can only amplify the question of the tomb" in Derrida's work. Riddel's assertions draw attention to Derrida's notion that a crypt is *built* by violence. I also have in mind Mark Wigley's assertion that the crypt "directs attention to the implicit violence of architecture by identifying the subtle mechanism with which a space can conceal the precise but elusive geometry of concealment that produces the effect of space by orchestrating a

sustained double violence" (147). Riddel's exclusion of Madeline
Usher from his discussion poses the question of the tomb by
recapitulating Roderick Usher's entombment of his twin. Our attention is drawn to the violence of the attempt to maintain rigid limits
or boundaries through radical exclusion. Similarly, each writer
draws attention to the threat implied in the proximity of what
might be called the "jettisoned object," a term Kristeva uses to
describe whatever "draws [one] toward the place where meaning
collapses" (*Powers of Horror* 2). Joseph Riddel's exclusion of
Madeline Usher from his discussion mimes Roderick Usher's
emtombment of his sister, Madeline. Riddel's omission bears traces
of Usher's hysteria and anticipation of his sister's return from the
tomb. To take it even further, Riddel's omission can draw attention
to an aesthetics predicated upon exclusion, prohibition, repudia-
tion, and elimination. It also suggests that what is excluded is
"disgusting," a designation generally reserved for the "feminine"
or the "maternal." The subversion of this aesthetic is arguably
central to Gothic horror in general and, more specifically, to both
Derrida and Poe whose texts consistently draw one towards the
place of collapsed meaning evoked by Kristeva.

  In *Of Grammatology*, for example, Derrida examines the way
in which women's power is the "paradigm of violence and political anomaly" (176) hence the perceived necessity of containing
it, and women, "within domestic government" such that "woman
takes her place, remains in her place" (178). This notion draws
attention not only to what makes the "House of Usher" – text,
mansion, patronym – "a form of violence" but also to that which
subverts those forms by encroaching on certain borders: Madeline
Usher's return from the crypt, for example, seems analogous to
the effects produced by the workings of Derrida's *Glas*. Like the
"House of Usher," *Glas* concerns itself with the staging of contamination and disintegration and, thus, necessarily, with the
"feminine." In these terms, the feminine poses a threat to a certain
order, not because it is synonymous with "woman" – Derrida
cautions against mistaking the feminine for "a woman's femininity, for female sexuality" ("Choreographies" 163) – but because
it is unrepresentable. In other words, a warning is in effect not
to essentialize the "feminine" but to understand it as that "which
will not be pinned down by truth" (163). Of course, to some, this
notion is monstrous.

GLAS: STAGING CONTAMINATION,
A TERATOLOGY A.K.A PARASITE LOST

Van Helsing: "Do you not see how, of late, this monster has been creeping into knowledge experimentally?"

Count Dracula: "There is work to be done."

Bram Stoker, *Dracula*

According to Derrida, to stage contamination is to do "something altogether other than mixing literature and philosophy."[1] To stage contamination is to risk something: "Theatricality must traverse and restore 'existence' and 'flesh' ... Thus whatever can be said of the body can be said of the theater."[2] It is to open into the place where meaning, order, and identity collapse. It is to invite the touch that disturbs the borderline. Nearness, proximity, contiguity are all watchwords when contamination – from *contaminare* (to defile) which finds its root in *tangere* (to touch) – is at stake. To stage contamination is to acknowledge kinship, to invite consanguinity, even to create a hybrid, an abomination, a monster, if you will.

Glas is such a staging. It reads like a novel, a poem, a legend – the whole thing in plural translation, multiple, simultaneous, and productive. As a rebus, it gives the story of haunting and encryption:
... to be read in a topography that, like the crypt in the Self, is "twice cleft." Each column written towards

The vampire: "a pair of spring-controlled doors cut into the scenery, which allowed the fiendish Ruthven to disappear through apparently solid walls."[13] Staging the vampire: depending on its placement on the stage the trap "made the actor alternately body and spirit."[14] The trap enabled the vampire to rise through the stage floor or "through invisible doors in the flats, allowing him to make imperceptible, phantomlike intrusions into or out of domestic space."[15]

When the emphasis is on the body as the ground, sacrilege has a social nature. When somebody dies, the presence of the corpse, with its threat of imminent decay, occasions fear at the power of corruption, says Bataille.[16]

The corpse is death and it shows me the borders of my condition. Kristeva: "as in true theater, without makeup or masks."[17]

What does it mean to break this structure of belonging? An instrument of domestic disembodiment on the stage of the dream: "A new epiphany of the supernatural and the unconscious of the other, the borderline that divides them always permeable, without any privileging of either: "Of the remain(s), after all, there are, always, [says Derrida,] overlapping each other, two functions."[3] A theatre of cruelty?

This movement is not without violence. Rupture. Dislocation. Bring your tools to work. Two interpretations of interpretation: monstrous.[4] To stage contamination is to demonstrate the instability of the borders determining social identity, namely genealogy, filiation, sanguinity: the family *line*, if you will. Just ask Madeline Usher. Written from such a fault line, *Glas* undoes certain textual markers that determine identity. Of *Glas*, Peggy Kamuf says, "there are no notes, no chapter headings, no table of contents. Each column begins in what appears to be the middle of a sentence and ends, 283 pages further on, without any final punctuation. 'What is going on here?'"[5] The sentences with which *Glas* "ends" are conceivably the "beginnings" of the sentences with which the work opens. The sentence beginning with "What I had dreaded, naturally, already, republishes itself. Today, here now, the debris of [débris de]" on page 262 can be understood to circle back (round) to complete itself on page 1 with "*'what remained of a Rembrandt torn into small, very*

the divine must occur within cruelty."[18]

But limits are always passed by fantasy. What inscribes limits is always a question of ontology *and* desire. As a rebus, it is a story of haunting and encryption, both cause and effect. A tomb(stone) always marks a plot: the remains of the proper name in stages of decomposition.

In Derrida's *Glas*, as in Poe's "The Fall of the House of Usher," the body remanded to the tomb is still alive. When tampered with, the family tomb reveals its remains. Here, a crypt marks a passage: the desire to save from death.

"What remains of a signature?"[19]

This movement is not without violence.

A caveat in the form of a note from Mina Harker addressed to Abraham Van Helsing: "'Look out for D. He has just now, ... come from Carfax hurriedly and hastened toward the south. He seems to be going the round."[20]

To Van Helsing: "What do you make of that mark on her throat?"[21] From Dr. Seward's diary, recalling the words of Van Helsing: "'I have studied, over and over again since they came into my hands, all the papers relating to this monster [D]; and the more I have studied, the greater seems the necessity to utterly stamp him out ... He had a mighty brain, a learning beyond compare, and a heart that knew no fear and

regular squares and rammed down the shithole' is divided in two."[6]
"A writing that was not structurally legible – iterable – beyond the death of the addressee would not be writing."[7]
The same holds true for the left-hand column where the sentence, "But it runs to its ruin [perte], for it counted without [sans]," appears to end page 262 while page 1 begins, "what, after all of the remain(s), today, for us, here, now, of a Hegel?" To read *Glas* one must move circuitously, but around two columns, each one swallowing its own "tail" in a peristaltic gesture of incorporation.
How to "read" (*swallow*) when one could "begin" anywhere presided over by the figure of eternal return? Similarly, writing in each of two columns, which form circles of their own in another axis, impinges on the other, negotiating between what might have been contradictory discourses, moving across passages, performing "autotranslations," performing "the borderless condition of texts, and their susceptibility to the most unexpected encounters."[8]
Van Helsing: "'Do you not see how, of late, this monster has been creeping into knowledge experimentally? ... All the time that so great child-brain of his was growing."[9]
Child's play? Derrida "with a glance towards childbearing": what is at stake in the "irreducible differences"[10]

no remorse. He dared even to attend the Scholomance, and there was no branch of knowledge of his time that he did not essay ... He is experimenting, and doing it well; and if it had not been that we have crossed his path he would be yet – he may be yet if we fail – the father or furtherer of a new order of beings, whose road must lead through Death, not Life."[22]
"And what rough beast, its hour come round at last,/Slouches towards Bethlehem to be born?"[23]
Wayne Booth (seconded by M.H. Abrams): the "deconstructionist reading of a given work is plainly and simply parasitical on the obvious or univocal reading."[24]
One (column) negotiates the other in itself as an alien body. A crypt takes place. But where?
"She can project herself into my body and take command of it. She has a parasite soul; yes, she is a parasite, a monstrous parasite. She creeps into my frame as the hermit crab does into the whelk's shell. I am powerless."[25]
The requirement of a centre is in itself a kind of myth. The function of a centerer is mythological, always designating presence, origin, subject. Absence of centre is absence of both subject and author, says D. "Play," however, is "the disruption of presence."[26] The play of interpretation of interpretation today is doubled: "one seeks to decipher, dreams of deciphering a truth or an origin,"

rising from two interpretations of interpretation: "*conception, formation, gestation,* and *labor* ... I employ these words ... also with a glance toward those who, in a society from which I do not exclude myself, turn their eyes away when faced by the as yet unnamable, which is proclaiming itself and which can do so, as is necessary whenever a birth is in the offing, only under the species of the nonspecies, in the formless, mute, infant, and terrifying form of monstrosity."[11]

"I begin with love."[12]

while on the other hand, the other, "which is no longer turned toward the origin, affirms play and tries to pass beyond man and humanism, the name of man being the name of that being who, throughout the history of metaphysics or of onto-theology – in other words, throughout his entire history – has dreamed of full presence, the reassuring foundation, the origin and the end of play."[27]

"Yet I saw crypts when I looked at him."[28]

THE EXCLUSION OF THE DISGUSTING

To speak of the disgusting is to draw attention to what makes aesthetics possible. "Woman," for her association with the feminine, is often a site of repulsion. As Mark Wilgley points out, both Kant and Rousseau maintained that "woman is the figure of the dispossession of the authority of immediate expression by the mediations of representation. She is a double figure: the paradigm of nature when domesticated in the house and the paradigm of the alienation from nature when outside the house, untamed" (135). Wigley draws attention to the relationship between aesthetics – which he says, "is defined by its exclusion of the disgusting" (139) – and the threat of woman as polluting object. To link aesthetics with disgust and repulsion, Wigley draws upon Freud's notion of latency, arguing that disgust and shame are learned by the child:

this defensive mechanism of repulsion is erected during the "latency" period in which the child ... is trained to sublimate its original perversions with feelings of "disgust, feelings of shame, and the claims of aesthetics and moral ideals." In these terms, aesthetics is a defensive mechanism of repression that excludes whatever disgusts by forcing the effacement of the distinction between presentation [reality] and representation [imagination]. (142–3)

If aesthetics is a "defensive mechanism of repression," what does it defend against? It is telling that in a discussion of such an aesthetics,

Wigley never directly mentions the maternal, although he alludes to it in his claim for the feelings of disgust and shame sublimated by the "child." Against what threat do nausea and disgust defend? These are questions consistently taken up by Derrida in a writing that rigorously points up the limits as well as the necessity of borders. According to Mark Wigley, the danger is borderlessness: "that which is threatening is that which cannot be localized, that which cannot be placed either inside or outside an enclosure" (182). But here Wigley appears to be inhabiting a haunted "enclosure" similar to the one occupied by Roderick Usher in his desire to ward off what is "threatening." Wigley's avoidance demonstrates Kristeva's point that what must be excluded is that which "does not respect borders, positions, rules" (*Powers of Horror* 4).

What is common to both aesthetics and the Gothic (especially horror) is the concept of a border, the function of which is protection against what is "improper" or "unclean." As Barbara Creed argues, this protective border "is central to the construction of the monstrous in the horror film; that which crosses or threatens to cross the 'border' is abject" (10–11). While the exclusion of the disgusting to the "outside" is the founding movement of aesthetics, that same exclusionary movement in the Gothic as well as in cryptomimesis becomes the occasion for staging transgression and contamination.

In Bataille's view, repugnance and horror are linked to the opening of the "void" (59) yet are the "mainsprings of desire" (59). In Kristeva's view "defilement" and abjection are linked to the maternal. More specifically, Kristeva claims that the exclusion of the disgusting can be linked to maternal abjection and the child's struggle to achieve a separate existence as a "subject [who] will always be marked by the uncertainty of his borders" (*Powers of Horror* 63). Kristeva's argument that a whole area of religion concerns itself with the perils implicit in this relation indicates how fraught it can be maintaining the borders of an "I" whose identity is in danger of being subsumed either by the "void" or, in her lexicon, by the "maternal":

This is precisely where we encounter the rituals of defilement and their derivatives, which, based on the feeling of abjection and all converging on the maternal, attempt to symbolize the other threat to the subject: that of being swamped by the dual relationship, thereby risking the loss not of a part (castration) but of the totality of his living being. The function of these religious rituals is to ward off the subject's fear of his very own identity sinking irretrievably into the mother. (*Powers of Horror* 64)

Although speaking here of the link between religious rites and the abject, Kristeva's notion of "being swamped" and the threat to the identity of the subject can also shed light upon the dynamic relationship between Gothic horror and aesthetics, an association that is roughly analogous to the correspondence between cryptomimesis and aesthetics. These "pairs" all concern themselves not only with the concept of the border or with the threat of "defilement" that border-crossings imply but also with the "threat to the subject ... of being swamped." This threat comes about through an encounter with a certain *atopos* that we might think of as the "maternal," or the "void" but which, when speaking of cryptomimesis, seems most appropriately described by Barbara Creed as "the monstrous-feminine."

In her discussion of the horror genre, Barbara Creed argues that even though "the specific nature of the border changes ... the function of the monstrous [feminine] remains the same – to bring about an encounter between the symbolic order and that which threatens its stability" (11). Kristeva would be quick to point out that even though the horror genre often literalizes the disgusting – Barbara Creed lists walking corpses and bodily disfigurements, and says that "images of blood, vomit, pus, shit, etc. are central to our culturally/socially constructed notions of the horrific" (13) – that "it is "not lack of cleanliness or health that causes abjection but what disturbs identity, system, order" (*Powers of Horror* 4). In effect, an encounter with a text that threatens the symbolic order threatens identity. This threat is what Kristeva refers to when she asks, "how can I be without border?" (4). The emphasis of Kristeva's question should be placed on the "I" since it is a question of identity which resonates for the subject. To speak of a threat to the subject is to speak of abjection. To consider abjection is to consider the terror that the threat of borderlessness inspires.

In Poe's story, the twin figures of Madeline and Roderick Usher function as synecdoche for the abject. Madeline Usher, on the one hand, inspires in Roderick Usher what Kristeva would call "a terror that dissembles" (4) but she also figures as that which he must exclude – that is, keep *without* – in order to live. Upon her crossing the threshold, he falls dead to the floor, not because she has done him any physical violence, but because he has fallen "victim to the *terrors he had dreaded*" (Poe 547). Such terror is what Kristeva refers to in her discussion of the abject and its affect, particularly in the presence of a

corpse (or cadaver: *cadere*, to fall) that which has irremediably come a cropper, is cesspool, and death; it upsets even more violently the *one who confronts* it as fragile and fallacious chance. A wound with blood and pus, or the sickly, acrid smell of sweat, of decay, does not *signify* death. In the presence of signified death – a flat encephalograph, for instance – I would understand, react, or accept. No, as in true theater, without makeup or masks, refuse and corpses *show me* what I permanently thrust aside in order to live ... There, I am at the border of my condition as a living being ... If dung signifies the other side of the border, the place where I am not and which permits me to be, the corpse, the most sickening of wastes, is a border that has encroached upon everything. (*Powers of Horror* 3)

But what if the corpse should return from the grave? In crossing the threshold, Madeline Usher shows her twin what he has tried to "thrust aside in order to live." His sister's return from the crypt ushers *him* "toward the place where meaning collapses" (2). In this case, that place is the threshold, a word that recalls what Kristeva describes as the "*border* of [one's] condition as a living being" signifying, as Kristeva says, "the place where I am not and which permits me to be" (3). That Usher's "death" comes about through the collapse of certain borders can be understood in light of Barbara Creed's remarks about the abject's threat to life. Citing Kristeva, Creed remarks:

the abject threatens life; it must be "radically excluded" (Kristeva, 2) from the place of the living subject, propelled away from the body and deposited on the other side of an imaginary border which separates the self from that which threatens the self. Although the subject must exclude the abject, the abject must, nevertheless, be tolerated for that which threatens to destroy life also helps to define life. Further, the activity of exclusion is necessary to guarantee that the subject take up his/her proper place in relation to the symbolic. (9)

The "imaginary border" is integral to the distinctions between "inside" and "outside." These distinctions in turn determine "the place of the living-subject." Cryptomimesis demonstrates not only how ambiguous the distinctions between inside and outside can be but also how the ontological security of the so-called subject is threatened with multiple and vertiginous displacements to those distinctions. Barbara Creed demonstrates that the border, and the threat to its stability by the encroachment of the "disgusting," is fundamental to the concept of the abject and thereby to aesthetics which relies on exclusion of the disgusting.

In *Aporias* Derrida draws attention to the functioning of these divisions and also to the crossing of certain lines or borders which constitute a threat to identity:

An indivisible line. And one always assumes the institution of such an indivisibility. Customs, police, visa or passport, passenger identification – all of that is established upon this institution of the indivisible, the institution therefore of the step that is related to it, whether the step crosses it or not. Consequently, where the figure of the step is refused to intuition, where the identity or indivisibility of a line ... is compromised, the identity to oneself and therefore the possible identification of an intangible edge – the crossing of the line – becomes a *problem*. There is a *problem* as soon as the edge-line is threatened. And it is threatened by its first tracing. (11)

There is a *problem* as soon as the edge-line is threatened because, as Derrida suggests, threat is the necessary *condition* of any "first tracing." It is the threat itself which permits identity, system, and order. In these terms, the crossing of the line becomes a problem because it is the line that gives rise to the very notion of crossing.

WRITING ON THE THRESHOLD OF UNDECIDABILITY

In the preceding section, what became apparent was the way that the words *threshold* and *door* come into play as markers to alert us that we are *drawing near* a border such as that described by Kristeva, or to the "edge-line" as mentioned by Derrida. In Poe's and Derrida's work, do thresholds and doors serve as markers of desire? Do they indicate the site of a crypt where something must be kept safe? Consider for a moment the narrator's comments in Poe's story that he and Roderick Usher, having entombed Madeline Usher, "secured [behind them] the door of iron" (543). Here, the word *secured*, rather than merely *closed*, suggests that it is not enough to simply fasten the door. A secured door also carries with it the notion of protecting, guarding, defending. What is behind the door had better stay there.

Similarly, in another moment of uncanniness, the narrator glimpses the resemblance between the twins, Roderick and Madeline. He regards the sight of the latter, however, with "an utter astonishment not unmingled with dread" before being "oppressed" by "a feeling of stupor ... as a door, at length, closed upon her exit" (537). It seems that until the door closes upon Madeline's exit, forming a separation between her and him, the narrator is held in thrall to something dreadful and inexplicable. He cannot be freed from the torpor that overwhelms him until the door comes between them. Similarly, while awaiting his sister's approach from the tomb, Roderick Usher sits "with his face to the door," while the narrator reads to him. Hearing the opening of the coffin, he shrieks in anticipation of "the terrors he had dreaded":

Said I not that my senses were acute? I *now* tell you that I heard her first feeble movements in the hollow coffin. I heard them – many, many, days ago – yet I *dared not speak*! And now – tonight – Ethelred – ha! ha! – the breaking of the hermit's door, and the death-cry of the dragon, and the clangor of the shield! – say, rather, the rending of the coffin, and the grating of the iron hinges and her struggles within the coppered arch-way of the vault! ... *I tell you that she now stands without the door!* (547)

It is significant that standing without the *double* door is Roderick's *twin*, Lady Madeline of Usher, who completes and collapses the doppelgänger effect when the door bursts open; that is when *she* stands *without* the door. In this context, it is also interesting to consider that while the word *usher* denotes "one who is acting as a door-keeper," and that the verb form means "to precede," the word is derived from the Latin *ostium*, a door – extending from *os* for mouth – and thus draws our attention to the relationship between architecture and incorporation. As readers of Poe's story, we are simultaneously being drawn into and barred from an uncanny space, the like of which evokes a sense of what Derrida calls in "*Fors*," "a very specific and peculiar place, highly circumscribed, to which access can nevertheless only be gained by following the routes of a different topography" (xiii). Indeed, Usher's friend, the narrator seems very articulate on these Derridean "routes of a different topography":

I entered the Gothic archway of the hall. A valet, of stealthy step, then conducted me, in silence, through many dark and intricate passages in my progress to the studio of [Roderick Usher] ... While the objects around me – while the carvings of the ceilings, the sombre tapestries of the walls, the ebon blackness of the floors, and the phantasmagoric armorial trophies which rattled as I strode, were but matter to which, or to such as which, I had been accustomed from my infancy – while I hesitated not to acknowledge how *familiar* was all this – I still wondered to find how *unfamiliar* were the fancies which ordinary images were stirring up. On one of the staircases, I met the physician of the family. His countenance, I thought, wore a mingled expression of low cunning and perplexity. He accosted me with trepidation and passed on. The valet *now threw open a door and ushered* me into the presence of his master. (535, emphasis mine)

As this passage suggests, all of the designations of "usher," including its function as a proper name which inherits, suggest that Poe's text produces the idea that there is an "interior" that is somehow accessible through a door. And although he is commenting on Derrida's essay, "Before the Law," Mark Wigley's remarks can also be used to illuminate just such an opening:

The law is ... explicitly a space, literally an interior accessible through a door, and the "before" [*devant*] is ... both spatial and temporal, or, more precisely, in Derrida's reading [of Kafka], it is the spacing that comes before the space of the law. The "before" is like that of the title positioned before the text: neither inside nor outside it (such that Kafka's [and, for my purposes, Poe's] title reproduces what it describes). As Derrida points out, the space in the story turns out to be "empty." The law cannot be found beyond the door. It is not simply "in" the space but is encrypted by its markers. The essence of the law, which is to say, of the space, turns out to be its violation by spacing, a violation that is always hidden, "always cryptic." The door is therefore "an internal boundary opening on nothing." The space it marks is no more than the maintenance of this "secret." The origin of the law is "safeguarded" by the space, not by being hidden within it but by being hidden by the space itself, which is to say, by the representation of a space. *It is the very idea that there is an interior that encloses the secret.* (152, emphasis mine)

What Poe's work anticipates and where it intersects with Derrida's is in "the very idea that there is an interior that encloses the secret." What they share is a concern with "the representation of interior made possible by an ongoing repression" (Wigley 152). In Poe's case, the door is a cryptic marker that produces the idea of interiority and exteriority by drawing attention to the border that marks the divisions between the two: a threshold which is a hymeneal as well as a cryptic division. In Derrida's case, the crypt marks this division: "what the crypt commemorates [says Derrida], as the incorporated object's 'monument' or 'tomb,' is not the object itself, but its exclusion, the exclusion of a specific desire from the introjection process: A door is silently sealed off like a condemned passageway inside the Self, becoming the outcast safe" ("*Fors*" xvii).

The notion of threshold is important since it draws attention to the function of a border. But it is also significant because it gives us insight into a writing practice that produces what might be called a "borderline" subject. By staging a radical resistance to any rigorous determination of borders – including the question of the relation between texts – while continuing to trace along their edges, both Poe and Derrida can be considered as *writing on a threshold*. For example, in "Living-On: Border Lines," Derrida writes:

I wish to pose the question of the *bord*, the edge, the border, and the *bord de mer*, the shore. ... The question of the borderline precedes, as it were, the determination of all the dividing lines that I have just mentioned: between a fantasy and a "reality," an event and a nonevent, a fiction and a reality, one corpus and another, and so forth ... I shall perhaps endeavor to create an effect of *superimposing*, of superimprinting one text on the other ... What about this "on," this "*sur*," and its surface? An effect of superimposing: one procession is superimposed on the other, accompanying it without accompanying it. (256–7)

To write *on* a threshold, therefore, is to ask continuously, as Derrida does, "What are the borderlines of a text? How do they come about?" (258). Such questions call attention to the way that cryptomimesis stages what Peggy Kamuf refers to as "the question of the relation between texts once their limits or borders can no longer be rigorously determined" (255). Derrida's questions also point to the way that such staging produces a "borderline" subject as a spectral effect of a certain tracing. We might call such a tracing a superimposition of (the name) "Derrida" upon (the name) "Poe," thus "accompanying it without accompanying it."

In borderline writing, the *topos* of the "I" achieves its uncanny resonance through a kind of doppelgänger effect similar to that evoked in/by "The Fall of the House of Usher." It is an effect produced by *drawing upon* what Derrida refers to as "the border-line" ("Living On" 256) that separates the enclosed narrative from the other. In short, the borderline subject is a textual effect of superimposition ("Living On" 258) and suggests that what is at stake in "ghost writing" is a careful and sustained tracing of the *other*. In Poe's story, the notion of borderlessness, if not borderline subjects, prevails. In his discussion of the collapse of the distinction between the family and its residence in the minds of the peasantry, Joseph Riddel writes, "all differences, natural or cultural, are in a state of collapse or degeneration." He continues (at first quoting Poe's narrator):

"the quaint and equivocal appellation of the 'House of Usher'" signifies the irreversible direction of exhaustion and decay that predicates a final collapse of the distinctions between nature and culture, or material and spiritual, in the collapse of proper signification itself. It is the idea of the "direct" unbroken "line" of a teleological (and hence a narrational) order that is broken in this incompatible "house." The house of fiction reflects the "malady" in the fiction of the house. (130–1)

The house of fiction and the fiction of the house: how to get into it?

These terms draw attention to a kind of writing that is concerned with architecture, and in particular, as I mention above, with doors and thresholds. If writing on the threshold brings to mind the plank or stone at the bottom of a door that marks the divisions, borders, or boundaries between inside and outside, as well as between rooms, it also implies the sense of crossing a line. Here the attendant meanings of *cross* also come into play. It can denote a stake with a transverse bar, a trial or affliction, and a hybrid form of interbreeding or, in the case of plants, fertilization. As a verb the word *cross* suggests misunderstandings – to be at cross-purposes – as well as translations and transferences. Used adverbially, cross means intersecting, passing from side to side, and contrary or opposed. A writing that is cross-determined mounts a resistance to what Peggy Kamuf refers to as "the complementary beliefs that a text (1) has identifiable limits or borders and (2) exists in a stable system of reference to other texts of 'information' (its 'context') which, ideally at least, can be fully represented, for example through a scholarly apparatus of notes" (255). To a certain extent, then, Poe's and Derrida's writing practices pose what Derrida refers to as "the question of the *bord*, the edge, the border" ("Living On" 256), which is another way of addressing the question of the text – to explore what Joseph Riddel has called, "the collapse of proper signification itself" (130).

To pose the question of the text, one must always take the concept of borders, divisions, and boundaries into consideration along with the idea of their crossing. We can take our cue from Derrida's speculations on reading Freud's "apparently autobiographical point of view" as being inseparable from the discursive productions of the so-called analytic movement ("To speculate" 272). To read thus, says Derrida, "we must begin ... by pointing out in the hastily named 'internal' reading [of the writings of life death interlaced with autobiography, autography, and autothanotography], the places that are *structurally* open to *intersecting* with other net-works" (273, emphasis mine on the word *intersecting*). Derrida reminds us that whatever intersects must necessarily *cross*. Given the various meanings of the word *cross*, the notion of textual intersection becomes a complex issue that draws attention to its own indeterminacy, a point that Derrida takes up in his thinking on the iterability or citationality of the sign, the place of intentionality in the possibility of meaning, and the context as indeterminable, in any case.[29] Referring to what he calls "a law of undecidable contamination," Derrida argues for a rethinking of the entire field of signification in terms of the displacement of the distinction between meaning based on a theory of the pure speech act or event as intentional, and the "parasitic," which the former excludes as being "non-serious." Following Derrida's contention that writing has long been considered "parasitical" by the philosophical tradition, Mark Wigley asserts that "the logic of incorporation turns out to be that of the parasite, the foreigner occupying the domestic interior and unable to be expelled from it ... without ruining the space" (179). It is thus that Derrida's argument for contamination as an "internal and positive condition of possibility" ("Signature Event Context" 103) of signification in any case, finds its way into cryptomimesis as the model and the method of writing predicated upon a "law of undecidable contamination." Under such a law, textual intersections, as well as translations and transferences, can be understood in terms of *crossings*, a point which Derrida alludes to when he says, "I leave the word 'crossing' to all its genetic or genealogical chances. A certain writing will make its bed in them" ("To speculate" 273).

A certain writing will take its chances, will, in effect, even be the *subject* of crossing, the manifestations of which appear in the uncanny intersections between Derrida and Poe who are as uncannily bound to each other as the "Envois" suggests Freud and Heidegger are: "They did not know each other, but according to me they form a couple... They are bound to each other without reading each other and without corresponding ... two thinkers whose glances never crossed and who, without ever receiving a word from one another, say the same. They are turned to the same side (191).

Perhaps, "without ever receiving a word from one another" it is the *letters* of Poe and Derrida – if not their "glances" – that have crossed (a certain threshold) and "say the same." When, in Poe's story Roderick Usher exclaims "Have I not heard her footsteps on the stair?" (547) we are given a sense of what Derrida means when, in *Aporias*, he remarks "the crossing of borders always announces itself according to the movement of a certain step [*pas*] – and of the step that crosses a line" (*Aporias* 11). To a certain extent, the affinity between Derrida and Poe and, for that matter, between Derrida and Stephen King, can be thought through the notion of the cross(ing), the border, and the threshold, all of which draw attention to themselves as dynamic sites of contamination, as uncanny loci of (often contradictory) translations, and most significantly, of living-death in the figure of return. In effect, the "border crossings" evoked by Derrida, Poe and King "say the same" – they all assert that death is at the heart of experience and that certain thresholds cannot be crossed without consequence.

A CRYPTIC SPACING:
THE DESTRUCTION
OF REPRESENTATION

In an essay entitled "Holbein's Dead Christ," Julia Kristeva examines Holbein's painting in which she perceives a spiritual crisis.

Kristeva claims this crisis ensues when Holbein leads us "to the ultimate edge of belief, to the threshold of nonmeaning" (263) where, she asserts, "*death* ... lies at the center of ... experience" (262). Kristeva claims that the painting is so disturbing because the viewer's death is implicated in the death of God and "there isn't the slightest suggestion of transcendency" (241). These ideas are equally fruitful for an examination of Derrida, Poe, or King for whom "the suggestion of transcendence" is also linked to the problem of representation which becomes one of *antisemantics*, a cryptic spacing that is the result of violence, contradiction, and pleasure. Kristeva could just as well be speaking of Derrida, Poe, or King when she remarks that "like Pascal's invisible tomb, death cannot be represented in Freud's unconscious. It is imprinted there, however ... by spacings, blanks, discontinuities or the destruction of representation" (265). Similarly, her interest in the way Holbein seems to have "given up all architectural or compositional fancy," suggests the painting achieves a level of mimesis that articulates, in a "self-conscious" way, the conditions of its own making (241).

The result is both peculiar and disturbing; as Kristeva says, "the tombstone weighs down on the upper portion of the painting, which is merely twelve inches high, and intensifies the feeling of permanent death: *this corpse will never rise again*" (241–2, emphasis mine). Kristeva's remarks suggest that in terms of mimesis, death has certain *spatial* problematics that can be thought through only in terms of the architecture of the crypt itself and that which it *houses*; usually a corpse that once buried, will stay that way – unless, of course, one can return from the dead.[30]

Like Holbein, Derrida also takes on the spatial problematics that death represents when he *mimes* in discourse a visual work. In "Cartouches," for example, Derrida *draws* upon Gérard Titus-Carmel's work entitled *The Pocket-Size Tlingit Coffin* (1975–1976) which consists of a sculpture – a mahogany box – and 127 drawings of this model, each from a different angle. When Derrida asks in "*Fors*," "What is a crypt? What if I were writing on one now?" (xi) and adds "not a crypt *in general*, but *this* one, in its singularity, the one I shall keep coming back to" (xiii), his comments suggest how cryptomimesis traces the surface of the object, be it literal or figurative. In "*Fors*" Derrida evokes a crypt – "this one" – and like the viewer in Holbein's painting, we stand both within and without the fantasy of that architecture's place. In short, we are *drawn* in.

But we have crossed a line. A writing in which "death lies at the center of experience" is a writing that problematizes space. Because it concerns itself with border crossings, a writing of this nature is always marked by contradiction.

But to return to the word *cross*. Although the word draws attention to itself in Christian terms of a promise and a sacrifice it also, paradoxically, gives us the sense of a "double cross" through which we are led to the site of betrayal, treachery, and cheating, perhaps even the scene of a crime, the clues to which, in the works of Derrida, Poe, and King, are determined by the anagrammatic ambiguity of words given us as infinite, multi-dimensionsal crossword puzzles comprised not only of words but also of words as things, parts of words, and words that *translate* the unspeakability of other words or letters. This process mimes the fantasy of incorporation which, according to Derrida, does not consist "in representing-hiding one word by another, one thing by another, a thing by a word or a word by a thing, but in picking out from the extended series of allosemes, a term that then (in a second-degree distancing) is translated into a synonym" ("*Fors*" xli–xlii).

RETURNING WITH A DIFFERANCE

Translated into synonyms, these words are as multiply determined as rebuses and, in a sense, mark the threshold between introjection and incorporation, between mourning and melancholy, so to speak. Written from a border, these texts *produce the crypt effect* which can also be understood as the vertigo that comes about from the multiple displacements in language; in terms of cryptomimesis such texts are like Holbein's painting: they give the impression of standing not only *without* "a door [that has been] silently sealed off like a condemned passageway inside the Self, becoming the outcast safe" *but also* of being positioned *within* an "outcast safe." In short, the crypt effect is one of continuous displacement in which the vacillating undecidability of one's position contributes to a reading and a writing of the text of the *other*, a notion which is suggested by Derrida's description of the crypt as a paradoxical "topography of inside outside."

In Derrida's writing, we are always being ushered to a threshold of undecidability. In such writing from the space between distinctions, cryptomimesis seeks to remember undecidability. It is thus anathema to "philosophical discourse" which "cannot master a word meaning two things at the same time and which therefore cannot be translated without an essential loss. Whether one translates *pharmakon* as 'poison' or 'remedy,' whether one comes down on the side of sickness or health, life or death, the undecidability is going to be lost" ("Roundtable on Translation" 120). Although cryptomimesis plays upon the undecidability of possible positions, staging, as it were, the specular play of language, it also draws attention to the figure of return (from the dead) in terms of legacy, transference, and correspondence. Where a return from the dead takes the form of iterability, it implies in reading/writing the text of the other that a particular economy is at work: a system of correspondence – what Derrida might call a postal system – because the figure of return also indicates a certain undeliverability, say of a letter which never reaches its destination; a structure which, in essence, interrupts the self-reflexivity of the hermeneutic circle. The writer of "Envois," reading Plato, recognizes the implicit risk of such an exchange:

"They are, in effect, numerous, those who ask me to write to them, and it is difficult to refuse them openly. My serious letters therefore begin with 'God,' theos, and those that are less so with 'the gods,' theoi." ... You can always run after the proof: as if I were saying to you, here it is, it is I who am speaking, and I am speaking to you, uniquely, each time that I write "you," it is true that I am addressing myself authentically to you, with full and true speech, presently. When I say "all of you" ["*vous*"], when I pluralize, it is that I am addressing myself less seriously to you, that my letter is not really destined to you, that it is not destined to arrive at its destination, for you are, yourself, my unique, my only destination. (136)

The writer of "Envois" plays upon a certain radical otherness, the structure of which corresponds to/with the uncanny doubleness of the ear and its ties to the crypt and the (living) dead. The link to be made, therefore, is not only between the ear and the crypt – in general and in particular – but also between the crypt, as a "vault of desire," and the text of the other, a vertiginous structure that the writer of "Envois" evokes while staging those cryptic love-letters:

and when I call you my love, my love, is it you I am calling or my love? You, my love, is it you I thereby name, is it to you that I address myself?

I don't know if the question is well put, it frightens me. But I am sure that the answer, if it gets to me one day, will have come to me from you. You alone, my love, you alone, will have known it.

...

when I call you my love, is it that I am calling you, yourself, or is it that I am telling my love? and when I tell you my love is it that I am declaring my love to you or indeed that I am telling *you*, yourself, my love, and that you are my love. I want so much to tell you. (8)

What is telling about this letter is the undecidability of its pronominal play. In a certain way, *it tells the other* by calling up ghosts, which in turn can suggest what is at stake in both Derrida's writing practice and in my own reading. Consider, briefly, Derrida's remarks on Marx's "obsession with ghosts" and his (Marx's) harrying of Max Stirner:

I have my own feeling on this subject (I insist that it is a *feeling, my* feeling and I have no reason to deny that it projects itself necessarily into the scene I am interpreting: my "thesis," my hypothesis, or my hypostasis, precisely, is that it is never possible to avoid this precipitation, since everyone reads, acts, writes with *his or her* ghosts, even when one goes after the ghosts of the other). (*Specters* 139)

Derrida's answer to his own question, "Why this hunt for ghosts?" his reflection on the question, leads me to consider the idiosyncrasies of "my" reading as well as the uncanny structure of textuality in general which, as I said earlier, the Gothic has always allegorized. Why this hunt for ghosts? As usual, Derrida's assertions are telling:

He [Marx/Derrida/me?] has recognized someone who, like him, appears obsessed by ghosts and by the figure of the ghost and by its names with their troubling consonance and reference (*Geist, Gespenst*). Someone who is besieged, like him, by the same and by another, by the same that is each time another, because the identity of the ghost is precisely the "problem" ... I am describing then this feeling: that of a Marx obsessed, haunted, possessed *like/as* Stirner, and perhaps more than him, which is even harder to take. (139–40)

This hunt for ghosts is one reason why cryptomimesis is always *memory* work, but the question arises, work in whose memory?

In "To Speculate – On 'Freud,'" Derrida suggests what is at stake in this ghostly memory work not only for "Freud" but also for "Derrida":

Which is Freud's devil? The one that he counterfeits, or that he represents as the devil's "advocate," doubtless in order to *defend* him judiciously, taking up his cause, the cause in the "something else" [*"autre chose"*] ... Which is the devil that impels Freud to write? What the devil by impelling him to write in sum writes in his place without ever writing anything himself? Is this to be analyzed beyond Freud's self-analysis? And what are Freud's "unknown words" which are written with another hand, also his own, at this strange feast? Which is the revenant? To whom, to what, and from whence will he come back [*revenir*]? It is in the future that the question will be asked. (271)

In "Derrida's" case, which is the revenant? Is it "my" reading? What has he sent? What, if anything, is being enclosed, walled up like the black cat in Poe's tale of the same name; the cat who was entombed with a murdered woman and whose howls and shrieks alerted the police to the tomb's existence and the ghastly corpse within? What, if anything, is being enclosed, like the corpse of the murdered man, concealed beneath the floorboards whose "tell tale heart" beat so haunted the murderer that he gave himself away to the police? Lastly, what, if anything, is being enclosed, buried alive like Madeline Usher, whose return from the copper-lined tomb brings down the house? If "Derrida" was the name of one of Poe's narrators, we might understand that Poe is already writing with "another hand" so as to return to himself *in secret* certain "unknown words" that take the shape of a certain architecture of desire:

Caulked or padded along its inner partition, with cement or concrete on the other side, the cryptic safe protects from the outside the very secret of its clandestine inclusion or its internal exclusion. Is this strange place *hermetically* sealed? The fact that one must always answer *yes* and *no* to this question ... will have already been apparent from the topographical structure of the crypt, on its highest level of generality: The crypt can constitute its secret by means of its division, its fracture. "I" can *save* an inner safe only by putting it inside "myself," *beside(s)* myself, outside. ("*Fors*" xiv)

Although we have come the long way around, we can now recall Derrida's remark with which I began this discussion on the economics of revanence: "it was *something very strange* which returned *utterly without me.*" Although, in the above passage, Derrida refers to the spatial and temporal condition of the fantasy of incorporation – "the secret of its clandestine inclusion or its internal exclusion" – his remarks emphasize the uncanniness of a writing that returns, like a revenant, *without* him, where the word "without" not only stages a radical spatial indeterminacy but also gives us to understand the uncanniness that comes about in the wake of sending. This ambivalence is what the writer of the "Envois" implies when he says "the condition for me to renounce nothing and that my love comes back to me, and from me be it understood, is that you are there, over there, quite alive outside of me. Out of reach. And that you send me back" (29).

In "Literature and the Right to Death," Blanchot uses the figure of a Lazarus to connect literature and politics, negation and language, to bring about a similar ambivalence. Blanchot describes this figure as the "Lazarus in the tomb, and not Lazarus saved, the one who already smells bad, who is Evil, Lazarus lost and not Lazarus saved brought back to life … Literature … dispenses with the writer … That is why it cannot be confused with consciousness, which illuminates things and makes decisions; it is *my* consciousness *without me*" (46–7). Is what returns then, another I? Or is it you? To the extent that the other is always bound to a determination of the "self," the emergence of such radical otherness occasions what Kristeva would call "a massive and sudden emergence of uncanniness, which, familiar as it might have been in an opaque and forgotten life, now harries me as radically separate, *loathsome*. Not me. Not that. But not nothing, either" (*Powers of Horror* 2). It is clear from Kristeva's remarks that a return of the other has a profound emotional import. In Stephen King's *Pet Sematary*, the return of the dead from the grave might be seen to materialize the *affect* implicit in both Blanchot's and Kristeva's remarks, since the horror they evoke appears predicated not only upon our apprehension of what Blanchot would call "beings deprived of being" (39) but also because, as corpses, they return *us* to "what [we] permanently thrust aside in order to live" (Kristeva, *Powers of Horror* 3).

Consider the following passages from Stephen King's novel which describe Louis Creed exhuming the body of his son Gage, in order to rebury it in the same ground from which the family cat, Church, returned from the dead:

The smell hit him first, and Louis recoiled, gagging. He hung on the edge of the grave, breathing hard, and just when he thought he had his gorge under control, his entire, big, tasteless meal came up in a spurt ... At last the nausea passed. Teeth clamped together, he took the flashlight out of his armpit and shone it down into the open coffin.

A deep horror that was very nearly awe stole over him ...

The moss [that was growing on Gage's skin] was damp but no more than a scum. He should have expected it; there had been rain, and a grave liner was not watertight. Flashing his light to either side, Louis saw that the coffin was lying in a thin puddle. Beneath the light slime of growth, he saw his son ...

He worked his arms under Gage. The body lolled bonelessly from side to side, and a sudden, awful certainty came over [Louis]: when he lifted Gage, Gage's body would break apart and he would be left with the pieces. He would be left standing with his feet on the sides of the grave liner with the pieces, screaming. And that was how they would find him ...

He got Gage under the arms, aware of the fetid dampness, and lifted him that way, as he had lifted him so often from his evening tub. Gage's head lolled all the way to the middle of his back. (341–3)

This description of the corpse is classic abjection material. As Kristeva says, the corpse signifies not one side but always "the other side of the border, the place where I am not and which permits me to be" (*Powers of Horror* 3). In the classic horror film, as Barbara Creed remarks, the figure of the animated corpse is so fearful, so "loathsome" (to use Kristeva's term) because it comes to us from the other side of the border, returning us to what we are *not*. The pervasiveness of this figure in popular culture demonstrates how powerful the draw of the border actually is: "one of the most basic forms of pollution – the body without a soul. As a form of waste it represents the opposite of the spiritual, the religious symbolic. In relation to the horror film, *it is relevant to note that several of the most popular horrific figures are 'bodies without souls' (the vampire), the 'living corpse' (the zombie), corpse-eater (the ghoul) and the robot or android*" (Creed 10).

I mentioned earlier that according to Creed, the concept of the border is integral to "the construction of the monstrous in the horror film" (11). The same holds true for the novel, of which Stephen King's is a case in point. Recall the warning given to Louis Creed by the student who dies in his arms: "Don't go beyond, no matter how much you feel you need to. The barrier was not meant to be broken." Although the presence of corpses evokes abjection on the part of the protagonist in King's novel, it is the animated corpse – the one so familiar to the Gothic, the one who returns from the grave as if summoned by the *refusal to mourn* – that materializes the collapse of meaning to which Kristeva refers.

If, as Bataille suggests, burial of the corpse – "that nauseous, rank and heaving matter, frightful to look upon, a ferment of life, teeming with worms, grubs and eggs [which] is at the bottom of the decisive reactions we call nausea, disgust or repugnance" (56) – keeps the *living* safe from the "contagion" of death, then the corpse's return from the grave in fiction and in film brings us to cryptomimesis – brings us edging towards the "void" that death occasions in the midst of life. What we have when the dead return from the grave in King's novel is a *staging* of the dynamic relationship that cryptomimesis evokes between desire and horror, between mourning and the refusal to mourn, a staging which – because it goes against what Freud calls the normal work of mourning – keeps the dead alive, keeps them returning, but with a "differance."

An Art of Chicanery

In *Art of Darkness: A Poetics of the Gothic*, Anne Williams explores the problem of language and multiple meaning in the Gothic. She contends that in the Gothic, "language is multifarious, duplicitous, and paradoxical" (67).[1] In terms of cryptomimesis, Williams's remarks suggest one of the convergences between the Gothic and Derrida's writing practice. They draw attention to a certain (poetic) encounter with language which is labyrinthine in that it admits the multiple and the ambiguous. Williams has something to say on this sort of labyrinthine writing that characterizes the Gothic:

Gothic conventions ... imply a fascination with the problem of language, with possible fissures in the system of the Symbolic as a whole. Most – perhaps *all* – Gothic conventions express some anxiety about "meaning." In Gothic, fragments of language often serve ambiguously to further the plot – in letters (lost, stolen, buried); in mysterious warnings, prophecies, oaths and curses; in lost wills and lost marriage lines. Such fragments may be misinterpreted (often because they are removed from the original context), and frequently deceive or betray the interpreter. (67)

Derrida may not be explicitly talking about the Gothic, but he might as well be for his "fascination" with "possible fissures in the system of the Symbolic." For Derrida, multiple interpretations spring from

playing with the allosemes and their synonyms (always more numerous in their open series than is indicated in a dictionary), [such writing] swerves off at an angle in order to throw the reader off the track and make its itinerary unreadable. An art of chicanery: judicial pettifogging, sophistic ratiocination, but also [*chicane* = maze] a topographical strategy multiplying simulated barriers, hidden doors, obligatory detours, abrupt changes of direction [*sens*], all the trials and errors of a game of solitaire meant both to seduce and to discourage, to fascinate, and fatigue. ("*Fors*" xlii)

To enter Derrida's text is to encounter the seductive, discouraging, fascinating, and fatiguing labyrinth. It is to enter upon writing that is essentially poetic, its folds multiple, productive of a simultaneity of meanings that "make [an] itinerary unreadable." The itinerary of a cryptomimetic text is unreadable because of labyrinthine detours that proliferate, rather than limit meaning, thus evoking, as the writer of "Envois" suggests, a kind of delirium in the face of the multiple:

Suppose that at the end of reading something, one of the voices of the book murmurs to you something like: every time I said "*arrive,*" I was thinking of you ... Not of what I expect *from you*, as if your coming were still an accident of yours, but of you, uniquely, you who arrive, who are what arrives, you who are for me what arrives, what comes to me from a single venue. The text then sees itself transfigured by this, they would have to reread everything, and the other texts from the beginning of time ... And if another voice in the same book says: everything is connoted in *do*, there are only the *dos* that count, look back over the entire scansion (not the *das* as in *fort/da* or derrida, but also the most trailing, drawling *dos*, like *derrière les rideaux* [behind the curtains]), then it would be necessary to go through everything once more, which is one more book. (78)

To go through everything once more is to be drawn into the infinite generation of texts. That is anathema to identity. To be caught up in the delirium of cryptomimesis is to participate in the ebbs, flows, currents, and undertows of its sea-changes: the always already pluridimensional condition of *differance* in language.

Oscillating between philosophy and literature, cryptomimesis undermines notions of authorship and style to make a break with originary meanings. Comprised of crazily angled organizing frames, cryptomimetic texts, like *Glas* or the "Envois," appear structured less on principles of "narrative" that engage us in totalizing gestures of interpretation than on the disjunctions of space and time that are characteristic of experimental video. To borrow a phrase from Fredric Jameson, Derrida's texts appear to be comprised of "fragments in flight" and function like a video text in that reading becomes an immersion in the "total flow of the thing itself" (78). It is not contradictory, however, to claim that cryptomimesis achieves an unreadable itinerary because it "swerves off at an angle" from what Cixous in "Sorties," refers to as "explanation, interpretation, and all the authorities pinpointing localization" (96). Not because it *discourages* explanation or interpretation, cryptomimesis, on the contrary, solicits it. That is, a cryptomimetic text does not resist the "incessant deciphering" of the will to power/interpretation but *invites* it by generating a power surge along the circuitry of desire. The effect is what Dennis Foster calls, "a kind of counterhegemony, not an escape from the structure of discourse and ideology but a turning and multiplying of them" (522). Such a multiplication, a counterhegemony is at stake for the institutions of reading when the borders of texts are no longer strictly determinable. Seduced and discouraged, fascinated and fatigued, we are drawn into interminable (textual) analysis. Nicholas Rand's comments on Derrida's reading and writing practice confirm this notion of production:

Derrida uses the semantic diversity as well as the phonetic and anagrammatic ambiguity of words (that is, *age-old poetic devices*) in order to demonstrate that (philosophical) texts are at cross-purposes with themselves. His readings [and writings] often yield one or more words whose transparent meanings in the text are treated as indications of the need for integrity [which is the aim of philosophy,] whereas their less obvious lexical, phonetic, syntactic, and typographical aspects are revealed as the text's own insidious hints of disintegration. (*Wolf Man's* lxvii, emphasis mine)

Derrida's "topographical strategies" recall the labyrinthine structure of language/being as proposed by Gilles Deleuze: "a labyrinth is said, etymologically, to be multiple because it contains many folds. The multiple is not only what has many parts but what is folded in many ways."² Indeed, one might well argue that, in its resemblance to the labyrinthine design of a "Gothic" structure, there is nothing so haunted as the multiple and nothing so susceptible to disintegration, even if it's only the reader's sense (*sens*) of direction. Hence, I want to suggest that an encounter with Derrida's "semantic diversity" draws us into the *condition* of what Paul de Man calls "true poetic ambiguity ... [which proceeds] from the deep division of Being itself" ("The Dead End" 237).

It is not difficult to draw an analogy between a reader who, to recall Derrida's remarks in the passage above, becomes thrown "off the track" and the heroine who becomes lost in the labyrinthine structure of a Gothic castle in a similar encounter with "multiplying simulated barriers, hidden doors, obligatory detours, abrupt changes of direction." One is led, in both cases, to a *thinking* towards what Derrida, in *Specters of Marx*, calls "learning to live." This is an uncanny task since, says Derrida, "it would be necessary to learn spirits" (xviii).³ To learn spirits, however, a distinction must be made between spirit and spectre, however unstable, since wherever the spectre appears, it is, says Derrida, a "phenomenal and carnal form of the [*thing* that is called] spirit" (*Specters* 6). His remark draws attention to how the trope of the living-dead stages in both popular culture and Derrida's writing, the manifestation of a certain spirit, one facet of which is the profound mourning brought about by the so-called death of God. Although such mourning might well be understood as a form of cultural nostalgia based upon the loss of meaning or presence considered in humanist terms,⁴ it also draws attention to what Blanchot refers to as the "death of philosophy," which, says Blanchot "has [for some years] been affirming or realizing its own end" (qtd. in *Specters* 36).⁵

It is not difficult to imagine, for example, how the current resurgence of the trope of the revenant in the fiction and film of popular culture draws attention to the way that the so-called death of philosophy is also an occasion for its return from the grave, which is what Derrida suggests when he addresses what he calls "a question of the philosophical 'spirit' ... heading the [funerary] march at the moment of its 'disappearance'" (*Specters* 36). In these terms, philosophy becomes, as Derrida says, its own "*revenant*; it itself haunts its own places more than it inhabits them" (36). It can be argued, therefore, that the fiction and film of popular culture, repetitiously concerned with themes of psychic phenomena, the supernatural, the forces of "evil," the return of the dead from the grave, can be considered as a cultural *effect* of what Blanchot refers to as "philosophy ... affirming or realizing its own end." In a certain sense, philosophy can see reflected in the return of the dead in popular culture its own funeral procession. Blanchot appears to refer to this effect when he remarks on

the sunset that from now on accompanies every thinker, a strange *funereal* moment which the philosophical spirit celebrates in an exaltation that is, moreover, often joyful, leading its slow funeral procession during which it expects, in one way or another, to obtain its *resurrection*. And of course, such an expectation, crisis and feast of negativity, experience pushed as far as it will go to find out what resists, does not touch only on philosophy. (qtd. in *Specters* 36)

Blanchot's discussion confirms that haunting belongs to the structure of thought. It also draws attention to how an entire generation is haunted by what Timothy Bahti and Richard Klein refer to in their introduction to a special issue of *Diacritics* as "the Ghost of Theology," "the remainder and reminder in our thought of categories we can no longer believe in but cannot fail to repeat, hollowly, mechanically, in a ghostly fashion. No new transformation of these categories has occurred which is not another disguise under which they may continue their familiar oppression" (1).

In *The Ego and Its Own*, Max Stirner evokes the workings of just such a ghost when he recounts what he perceives as an ontological shift from antiquity to the moderns in the "order of the world" – a kind of disenchantment which put the spirit over sense – from the *"world of things"* to the *"world of the spirit"* (27). Stirner points out that the production of the spiritual demands that to be ideal, spirit must be other-worldly, and a human being must necessarily be *less* than the pure spirit which then, as Stirner says, can "only be *outside* me" (33). Stirner's point is that the determination of a certain spacing opens itself to issues of haunting in recalling the fantasy of incorporation since, as Stirner points out, the "Spirit of God," at least according to the Western view, also "dwells *in* us" (35, emphasis mine).[6] That such spacing is accomplished, Stirner suggests, is shown in the fact that we make a distinction between "I" and "spirit." The hunger for the other world depends upon it. Stirner points out that even with the doubts which have been raised in the course of time against the tenets of Western religion, this spatial distinction remains integral:

If somebody told you you were altogether spirit, you would take hold of your body and not believe him, but answer: "I *have* a spirit, no doubt, but do not exist only as spirit, but as a man with a body." You would still distinguish *yourself* from "your spirit." "But," replies he, "it is your destiny, even though now you are yet going about in the fetters of the body, to be one day a 'blessed spirit,' and, however you may conceive of the future aspect of your spirit, so much is yet certain, that in death you will put off this body and yet keep yourself, your spirit, for all eternity; accordingly your spirit is the eternal and true in you, the body only a dwelling here below, which you may leave and perhaps exchange for another." (31)

Stirner argues that even if one no longer has faith in Western religion and no longer believes in the immortality of the spirit, one tenet still survives undisturbed: "that the spirit is your better part, and that the spiritual has greater claims on you than anything else" (31–2). Stirner points out that one still says "Spirits exist!" even though reason claims otherwise, a notion that is borne out by the revival of interest in the Gothic. What continues to haunt us, says Stirner, is "the mysterious spook that we call highest essence," (40) or the "Supreme Being,"[7] even though the very belief in God suffered by the laying aside of the belief in spirits and ghosts. Stirner points out that the Romantics were conscious:[8]

The Romantics were quite conscious what a blow the very belief in God suffered by the laying aside of the belief in spirits or ghosts, and they tried to help us out of the baleful consequences, not only by their reawakened fairy-world, but at last, and especially, by the "intrusion of a higher world," by their somnambulists, visionaries of Prévorst, etc. The good believers and fathers of the Church did not suspect that with the belief in ghosts the foundation of religion was withdrawn and that since then it has been floating in the air. He who no longer believes in any ghost needs only to travel on consistently in his unbelief to see that there is no separate being at all concealed behind things, no ghost or – what is naively reckoned synonymous even in our use of words – no "spirit." (35)

This passage from Stirner can help explain why Derrida makes the distinction between spectre and spirit. As Stirner's remarks suggest, we continue to live *in the spirit of* a haunted patriarchy which, since the Enlightenment, at least, has been marked by a profound (refusal) of mourning in the wake of the so-called death of God. (To the list of the departed, we could of course add the Author, History, Consciousness, and the Subject.)

The refusal to mourn takes the form of incorporation and takes the shape of a nostalgic veneration for both the past and for the conveying of "pastness," which is how Fredric Jameson refers to the nostalgia underlying the desperation of current collective and social attempts in fiction and film "to appropriate a missing past" (19). In these works (and in their critical reception), the return of the dead from the grave is a case in point, for it is not only represented as an occasion of horror, although this aspect necessarily remains intact, but also of regret, sadness, and melancholy. Slavoj Žižek has noted this trend in popular culture and provides an "archetypal" example of the current trend in the genre. Žižek describes George Romero's *Night of the Living Dead* as a film "where the 'undead' are not portrayed as embodiments of pure evil, of a simple drive to kill or revenge, but as sufferers, pursuing their victims with an awkward persistence, colored by a kind of infinite sadness (as in Werner Herzog's *Nosferatu*, in which the vampire is not a simple machinery of evil with a cynical smile on his lips, but a melancholic sufferer longing for salvation) (22–3)."[9]

As Žižek's remarks suggest, even the so-called monsters of popular culture suffer nostalgia for a time when salvation was an option. To live in the spirit of a haunted patriarchy is to suffer nostalgia and, therefore, to be *spoken*, which is what Derrida means when he says

everything is concentrated then in the German expression *es spukt*, which translations are obliged to circumvent. One would have to say: it haunts, it ghosts, it specters, there is some phantom there, it has the feel of the living-dead-manor house, spiritualism, occult science, gothic novel, obscurantism, atmosphere of anonymous threat or imminence. The subject that haunts is not identifiable, one cannot see, localize, fix any form, one cannot decide between hallucination and perception, there are only displacements; one feels oneself looked at by what one cannot see. (135–6)

Whereas Nicolas Abraham and Maria Torok would describe the phantom in terms of "the refusal to reclaim as our own the part of ourselves that we placed in what we lost" ("Mourning *or* Melancholia" 127), Derrida asserts that "humanity is but a collection or series of ghosts" (*Specters* 138). These comments bring forward the notion that we ourselves are spectres who, like Nosferatu, long for "salvation" in some form.[10] On the one hand the spectre is the "carnal apparition[s] of the spirit, its phenomenal body, its fallen and guilty body, [the spectre] is also the impatient and nostalgic waiting for a redemption, namely, once again, for a spirit (*auf Erlösung harrt, nämlich ein Geist*). [On the other hand] the ghost would be the deferred spirit, the promise or calculation of an expiation" (136). To a certain extent, the "spirit" incarnates in the "phenomenal body" of "writing" as well as that of a "subject" in a way that recalls the fantasy of incorporation:

In the flesh (*Leib*)! For there is no ghost, there is never any becoming-specter of the spirit without at least an appearance of flesh, in a space of invisible visibility, like the dis-appearing of an apparition. For there to be ghost, there must be a return to the body, but to a body that is more abstract than ever. The spectrogenic process corresponds therefore to a paradoxical *incorporation*. Once ideas or thoughts (*Gedanke*) are detached from their substratum, one engenders some ghost by *giving them a body*. Not by returning to the living body from which ideas and thoughts have been torn loose, but by incarnating the latter in *another artifactual body, a prosthetic body*, a ghost of spirit, one might say a ghost of the ghost. (126)

It is *in* this spirit that Derrida makes the assertion that "deconstruction" – roughly analogous to what I am calling cryptomimesis – takes place "in a certain *spirit of Marxism*" and that deconstruction, as such, "would have been impossible and unthinkable in a pre-Marxist space" (92). This notion suggests that deconstruction is the ghost or the deferred promise of (a certain spirit of) Marxism that is generationally specific:

There has been, then, this attempted radicalization of Marxism called deconstruction (and in which, as some have noted, a certain economic concept of the differantial economy and of exappropriation, or even of the gift, plays an organizing role, as does the concept of work tied to differance and to the work of mourning in general). If this attempt has been prudent and sparing but rarely negative in the strategy of its references to Marx, it is because the Marxist ontology, the appellation Marx, the legitimation by way of Marx had been in a way too solidly *taken over* [arraisonnées]. They appeared to be welded to an orthodoxy, to apparatuses and strategies, whose least fault was not only that they were, as such, deprived of a future, deprived of the future itself. By "welded" one may understand an artifactual but solid adherence whose very event constituted the whole history of the world for the last century and a half, and thus the whole history of my generation. (92)

It is significant that Derrida conceives of deconstruction and its relations to a certain spirit of Marxism in terms of the question of the phantom and of inheritance. These call attention to a writing practice that turns upon the fantasy of incorporation; they also draw attention to the moral and ethical implications surrounding Derrida's assertion (which I mention earlier) that the task of "learning to live" is difficult because "it would be necessary to learn spirits" (xviii). Learning to live brings with it the responsibility of an heir, says Derrida, and "whether we like it or not, whatever consciousness we have of it, we cannot not be [the heirs of Marx and Marxism]. There is no inheritance without a call to responsibility. An inheritance is always the reaffirmation of a debt, but a critical, selective, and filtering affirmation ... Even where it is not acknowledged, even where it remains unconscious or disavowed, this debt remains at work (91–2). That "this debt remains at work" even when it remains unconscious or disavowed draws attention to the workings of the phantom and its return as a deferred promise, an uncanny pledge upon which Gothic complications have always been predicated. Derrida's assertion that we must learn "*to make or to let* a spirit *speak*" (11) is also a *call* to responsibility that requires a certain thinking that we have yet to begin. It is one that Heidegger might say requires a thinking of *gathering* in the Old High German sense of the word *thing*, which according to Heidegger means, specifically, "a gathering to deliberate on a matter under discussion, a contested matter" ("The Thing" 174). Heidegger also points out that the Romans called a matter for discourse *res*:

The Roman word *res* designates that which concerns somebody, an affair, a contested matter, a case at law. The Romans also use it for the word *causa*. In its authentic and original sense, this word in no way signifies "cause"; *causa* means the case and hence also that which is the case, in the sense that something comes to pass and becomes due ... In English "thing" has still preserved the full semantic power of the Roman word: "He knows his things," he understands the matters that have a bearing on him; "He knows how to handle things," he knows how to go about dealing with affairs, that is, with what matters from case to case. (175)

I mention Heidegger in this context because it seems that when speaking of the "thing," he is implying a certain relationship, a "kinship" between thingness and thinking, a *thin(kin)g*, if you will. This is why Heidegger gives thought to "nearness" in how it implies a certain relationship – a reality – that scientific thought disavows or excludes.

What Heidegger evokes in his discussion in "The Thing," is the notion that thinking, as we know it, is a syntax that determines the spatial and temporal relationship between subject and object. In this sense, personal identity is, as Fredric Jameson suggests, first "the effect of a certain temporal unification of past and future with one's present; and second that such active temporal unification is itself a function of language, or better still of the sentence, as it moves along its hermeneutic circle through time" (26–7). Heidegger's description of the thingness of the jug – which he says "does not lie at all in the material of which it consists, but in the void that holds" ("The Thing" 169) – suggests that he is making an analogy between this kind of thinking and a certain relationship to language and, thus, writing that, in turn, draws attention to the "impalpable void" as the structuring principle of what "stands forth." Although Derrida seems often to take up where Heidegger left off, Derrida differs from Heidegger in that he is concerned to bring forward the uncanniness and the violence implicit in any kind of "structure" or institution. In these terms, language, thought, and the "subject" are all cryptically determined. This is why, in *Specters of Marx*, Derrida remarks that in terms of the Stirnerian ego, the "*living individual* would itself be inhabited and invaded by *its own specter*. It would be constituted by specters of which it becomes the host and which it assembles in the haunted community of a single body. Ego=ghost. Therefore 'I am' would mean 'I am haunted':

I am haunted by myself who am (haunted by myself who am haunted by myself who am ... and so forth). Whenever there is Ego, *es spukt*, 'it spooks.'" (133).

To be inhabited by spectres. To be constituted by spectres. Does not this ghostly assemblage suggest that the "living individual" is always already a revenant and that the Ego is, like the character Louis Creed in *Pet Sematary*, an effect of multiple hauntings that return from "the Unconscious *of* the other, according to what might be called the law of *another generation*" ("*Fors*" xxxi)? In this regard, the word "generation" is telling because it illustrates the return of the ghost or the revenant in terms of production, formation, engendering, and invention while at the same time rendering unstable any comfortable notions of intentionality which the "living individual" might entertain. This might be one reason why, as Nicholas Royle points out, "Derrida says that he feels like laughing every time he uses the word "unconscious" – especially with a possessive mark" (11). Such laughter is, of course, a recognition that "it spooks."

HOW TO SPEAK TO IT

In *Specters of Marx*, Derrida – who is using the figure of the scholar to demonstrate that thinking is *not* logic and *not* metaphysics – recalls Heidegger's insistence that a system emerges only when thinking comes to an end. As Heidegger sees it, thinking itself is poetic and since we do not take the poetic seriously, we have, paradoxically, *yet* to dwell in it. Instead, says Heidegger, we "dwell unpoetically" in a "curious excess of frantic measuring and calculating" ("Poetically Man Dwells" 228). Out of this "frantic measuring" appear the demarcations of both subject and object and, in turn, what Derrida would call scholars or spectators who, in positions of singularity, are incapable of a certain thinking that would "let a spirit speak." According to Derrida,

the thing [to speak to the specter] seems even more difficult for a reader, an expert, a professor, an interpreter, in short, for what Marcellus calls a "scholar." Perhaps for a spectator in general. Finally, the last one to whom a specter can appear, address itself, or pay attention is a spectator as such. At the theater or at school. The reasons for this are essential. As theoreticians or witnesses, spectators, observers, and intellectuals, scholars believe that looking is sufficient. (11)

That Derrida concurs with Heidegger, at least to a certain extent, is apparent in his remark that "thinking is what we already know we have not yet begun" (*Of Grammatology* 93). Instead, what we have are scholars – or subjects if you will – who insist on "the sharp distinction between the real and the unreal, the actual and the inactual, the living and the non-living, being and non-being … in the opposition between what is present and what is not" (*Specters* 11) and who, in effect, are not competent to let the spirit speak. This is because looking demands a certain perspective. But this is where the work of mourning – or cryptomimesis – comes in: a certain writing that draws us into the history as well as the production of the ghost. Writing, in this case, is learning to let the (plurivocal) spirit speak, a task which is the Gothic equivalent of pursuing a phantom through labyrinthine vaults, being led onwards by the echoes of footsteps which seem simultaneously to retreat in and advance from myriad directions.

Writing in *"Fors"* about the Wolf Man's range of associations and dissociations, Derrida's remarks also describe what awaits the reader who enters the labyrinthine structure of *his* writing:

The *Wolf Man's Magic Word* shows how a sign, having become arbitrary, can remotivate itself. And into what labyrinth, what multiplicity of heterogeneous places, one must enter in order to track down the cryptic motivation, for example in the case of *TR*, when it is marked by a proper-name effect (here, *tieret*), and when, consequently, it no longer belongs simply to the internal system of language. Such motivation does nevertheless function within the system and no linguistic consciousness can deny it. (xlvii)

Like the *Wolf Man's* system, cryptomimesis presents a challenge to the reader because it is *active*. Through the labyrinth of the ear, the sign is set in motion and remotivated. How to track it down? To recall Derrida, "its itinerary [is] unreadable" but not because it is incomprehensible, or "untranslatable" but because it multiplies, rather than attempts to reduce, meaning. It does so by leading the reader astray, encouraging her to wrangle over small details. It plays with the law of singularity, of identity, of meaning. It calls into question Man and the Subject. Cryptomimesis opens into spaces that have hitherto been disavowed: they are profane, mad, unconscious, feminine. This is why we can use Derrida's remarks about the Wolf Man's cryptonymy to describe his (Derrida's) writing practice: an "art of chicanery: judicial pettifogging or sophistic ratiocination" ("*Fors*" xlii). In that it *stages*, cryptomimesis is also an "act." Although Derek Attridge is talking about "the literary text, ... the signature ... the proper name, and the date being "an act" which he sees as "both a doing and an imitation of doing, both a performance and a record, both an event and a law" (19), his description applies just as well to the performativity of cryptomimesis. The reader who is seduced and fascinated can also become discouraged and fatigued through sheer undecidability: Which path to follow? What steps to take when I divides?

The architecture of the crypt draws us into thinking of what Paul de Man refers to as the division of Being which opens and multiplies in the wake of poetic "ambiguity" ("Dead End" 237). The shifting and multiple partitionings of the crypt bear witness to de Man's assertion that "poetry does no more than state and repeat [the] division [of Being]" (237). Because cryptomimesis plays upon the folds these "divisions" occasion – that is, upon the thetic relation to meaning or referent – it sets the stage for such an assembly by "multiplying simulated barriers, hidden doors, obligatory detours, abrupt changes of direction [*sens*], all the trials and errors of a game of solitaire meant both to seduce and to discourage, to fascinate, and fatigue" ("*Fors*" xlii).

WHAT DIVIDES IN THIS PLACE?

The game of solitaire, of course, falls to the reader who in turn is seduced, discouraged, fascinated, and fatigued each time the writing swerves off at an angle. Like the literary text, Derrida's [s]cryptograms set the stage for such an assembly. A crypt, says Derrida, is

not a natural place [*lieu*] but the striking history of an artifice, an *architecture*, an artifact: of a place *comprehended* within another but rigorously separate from it, isolated from general space by partitions, an enclosure, an enclave. So as to purloin *the thing* from the rest. Constructing a system of partitions with their inner and outer surfaces, the cryptic enclave produces a cleft in space, in the assembled system of various places, in the architectonics of the open square. ("*Fors*" xiv)

What does it mean to say that the crypt produces a "cleft" in space? Derrida delineates the spatial t(r)opography of the crypt by deploying the semantically plural word, *for*, which as Nicholas Rand points out "potentially [means] (when modified with the appropriate adjectives) the 'innermost heart' or 'conscience' (*le for intérieur*) and the 'temporal' or 'outward' jurisdiction of the church (*le for extérieur*). Derrida's use of the plural (*fors*) might indicate an amalgamation, but actually refers to another, prepositional meaning (namely, 'save,' 'except for,' 'outside of')" (*Wolf Man's* lxviii). By evoking denotative/connotative contradictions, these semantic shifts put undecidability into play in terms of slippages between distinctions of "inside" and "outside." This slippage is what Barbara Johnson suggests in a translator's note to "*Fors*," Derrida's foreword to Abraham and Torok's analysis of the Wolf Man: "The word *fors* in French, derived from the Latin *foris* (outside, outdoors), is an archaic preposition meaning 'except for, barring, save.' In addition, *fors* is the plural of the word *for*, which, in the French expression *le for interieur*, designates the inner heart, 'the tribunal of conscience,' subjective interiority. The word *fors* thus 'means' both interiority and exteriority" (xi–xii). Such play recalls Eve Kosofky Sedgwick's remarks in *The Coherence of Gothic Conventions* regarding the conventional structural topoi of the Gothic which function to codify how the fictional self is spatialized (12). Because the spatial conventions determine the division between inside and outside, they also draw attention to the dividing line itself as a border or a space that is *neither* inside nor outside.

The Gothic formula which Sedgwick evokes – "'an X within an X'" (20) or, better yet, "a story within a story within a story within a story" (19) – calls attention to the infinite *performativity* of that spacing. But it also recalls the structuring principle of cryptomimesis that is suggested by what Derrida says about the crypt and which I mentioned earlier: that it is "a place *comprehended* within another but rigorously separate from it, isolated from general space by partitions, an enclosure, an enclave ... a *safe*: sealed, and thus internal to itself, a secret interior within the public square [the forum], but, by the same token outside it, external to the interior" ("*Fors*" xiv).

What is kept "safe" in the "secret interior" is, of course, that which formed the crypt in the first place: "the double pressure of contradictory forces" ("*Fors*" xxiii) of desire. In architectural terms, the structuring principle of cryptomimesis is analogous to the fantasy of incorporation. It is meant to house something *other* and to keep it "safe." What is at work in Derrida's writing is the performativity of such a spacing which not only mimes the fantasy of incorporation but also draws the reader into the act which takes "place" in language.

Recalling Abraham and Torok on the subject of cryptic topography or topoi, he draws attention to the performativity of (cryptic) spacing: "What we will call (intrapsychic) *topos* is the condition in us that enables us to speak of any *place* whatsoever; we will call (intrapsychic) *force* that without which we would not understand any phenomenon of *intensity*.... These terms attempt the impossible: to grasp through language the very source from which language emanates" (xxxii).

To grasp through language the very source from which language emanates is to encounter the passe-partout, a term Derrida borrows from the nomenclature of framing. Derrida's remarks with respect to the *passe-partout* suggest what is at *work* in "constructing a system of partitions" as cryptomimesis:

One space remains to be broached in order to give place to the truth in painting. Neither inside nor outside, it spaces itself without letting itself be framed but it does not stand outside the frame. It works the frame, makes it work, lets it work, gives it work to do ... The trait is attracted and retrac(t)ed there by itself, attracts and dispenses with itself there ... It is situated. It situates between the visible edging and the phantom in the center, from which we *fascinate*. I propose to use this word intransitively, ... *Between* the outside and the inside, between the external and internal edge-line, the framer and the framed, the figure and the ground, form and content, signifier and signified, and *so on* for any two-faced opposition. The trait thus divides in "this place" where it takes place. ("Passe-Partout" 11–12)

I would argue that "what divides in 'this place'" is, for Derrida, (a) *displacement*, the type of (cryptic) division that recalls Eve Sedgwick's remarks regarding the "formal energy" upon which the Gothic formula – an X within an X – is predicated: "the focus of formal energy must be these strange barriers: how spontaneously they spring up and multiply, and what extremes of magic or violence are necessary to breach them" (20).

Sedgwick's discussion of formal energy is similar to the dynamic behind the structuring principle of what Abraham and Torok call "(intrapsychic) *force*" and what, in Derrida's case, I am calling cryptomimesis. If that writing practice is predicated upon the "formal energy" of what I argue could also be called *phantomime* – it finds its model and its method in the workings of the crypt where "the inner safe ... [places] itself outside ... or, if one prefers, [constitutes] 'within itself' the crypt as an outer safe. One might go on indefinitely switching the place names around in this dizzying topology (the inside as the outside of the outside, or of the inside; the outside as the inside of the inside, or of the outside, etc.)" ("*Fors*" xix). These spatial displacements articulate what is at stake as far as Derrida's writing practice is concerned. Certainly "*Fors*" can be thought of as Derrida's articulation of the principles of cryptomimesis itself.[11] The crypt (and for that matter, the *passe-partout)* functions as an allegory of writing that recapitulates what Derrida appears to glean from Abraham and Torok's insights on topography or topoi. Says Derrida, "we can see that these words [topography and topoi] must be taken neither literally nor figuratively but as an 'allusion to that without which no meaning – neither literal nor figurative – could come into being'" ("*Fors*" xxxii).

STRANGE BARRIERS

In a consideration of spacing as a discursive *effect* of language/writing, cryptomimesis reminds us, by staging it, of the law that binds violence to the production of an inside, be it of a text, a subject or an institution like "literature." The word *cleft*, that Derrida refers to, for example, denotes a space or division made by cleaving – that is, breaking, splitting – a violent movement resulting in a fissure or a split. This is the law of the production of an inside. In the formation of the thetic phase in the development of the subject, such a splitting produces the "spatial intuition" which, according to Kristeva, is "found at the heart of the functioning of signification" ("Revolution" 100). In the formation of the thetic phase, the mother, as the addressee of every demand, occupies the place of alterity. "She is, in other words, the phallus," says Kristeva. However, upon discovering the mother's "castration," the subject separates from fusion with the mother, thus ending the thetic phase which, asserts Kristeva, "posits the gap between the signifier and the signified as an opening up towards every desire but also every act, including the very *jouissance* that exceeds them" (101). Kristeva also makes the point that the "gap" between the signifier and signified is precisely "the break that establishes what Lacan calls the place of the Other as the place of the 'signifier.' The subject is hidden by an even purer signifier, this want-to-be confers on an *other* the role of containing the possibility of signification; and this other, who is no longer the mother ... presents itself as the place of the signifier that Lacan will call 'the Other'" (101). Where the Other refers to a hypothetical place or space, the Other is, therefore, the "place" in which is constituted the "I" who speaks "within" s/he who hears: also a crypt in the ear of the other. This spacing is always already a matter of sending, of the post, which is why the writer of "Envois" says, "in the beginning, in principle, was the post and I will never get over it" (29). In the beginning was not the word, but the post, the sending for which there is no address since the spacing, to a certain extent, precedes the sender. This is what Derrida means by "the first coming of the other" ("Mnemosyne" 22) and this is why the "Envois" proclaim, "you know everything, before me / you will always precede me" (19). This spacing is inextricably bound by the dialectics of desire as is suggested by Lacan who says, "if I have said that the unconscious is the discourse of the Other (with a capital O), it is in order to indicate the beyond in which the recognition of desire is bound up with the desire for recognition" ("Agency" 172).

This notion regarding the duality of desire and recognition illuminates Derrida's concern with alterity. For example, in *"Fors,"* Derrida's use of the word "enclosure" to describe the crypt's secret positioning "somewhere in a self" (xiv) draws attention to that uncanny "somewhere" as being the site of alterity in that the crypt is always already inhabited by an other. But such an uncanny spacing is already a condition of subjectivity. As Slavoj Žižek points out, "As soon as we wall or fence in a certain space [through enclosure], we experience more of it 'inside' than appears possible to the outside view" (35). In Derrida's case, where the word "enclosure" draws attention to its denotation – a space surrounded by walls or a fence – it also intimates, in *"Fors,"* the role of the Other as containing the possibility of signification. Likewise, in *Of Grammatology*, Derrida's remarks regarding the trace as "the opening of the first exteriority in general" (70) draw attention to subjectivity in terms of the other and of "spacing": "the enigmatic relationship of the living to its other and of an inside to an outside" (70).

Derrida points out that such relationships are, to us, "the most familiar thing in the world, as familiarity itself, would not appear ... without the nonpresense of the other inscribed within the sense of the present" (70–1). In fact, it is the "most familiar" and, therefore, uncanny, "nonpresence" of the other that enables the possibility of signification. In "Roundtable on Autobiography," Derrida suggests that the possibility of signification is also textual in nature in that "it is the ear of the other that signs. The ear of the other says me to me and constitutes the *autos* of my autobiography" (51). Similarly, in *Glas*, Derrida's concern with the dynamics of what constitutes the *autos* – textually, subjectively – is evoked in the relationship between text and space, between margin and inset and, finally, between columns of texts which problematize thetic referentiality by rendering unstable any distinctions between "inside" and "outside." In the "Envois," the speaker suggests what is at stake in terms of reading, writing, and interpretation: "Lacan already meant what I said, and myself I am only doing what he says he is doing. And there you are, the trick has been played, destination is back in my hand and dissemination is 'reversed' into Lacan's account" (151). In other words, Derrida's "trick" is also being played when *I* say "Derrida's remarks." In this sense, to play one's hand is to disturb the all too "familiar" attribution of "positions," of "place" that Derrida's use of the word "enclosure" suggests. Gregory Ulmer's reading of *Glas* illuminates such disturbances in thetic referentiality:

(Eventually I will write, "Derrida asks: 'What am I doing here?'" But the "I"s of *Glas* are never easily settled; they are multiple and mime the very text they are reading. I will oscillate between them, at times writing Derrida, at times I. But I do so without any assurance that this shorthand for an extremely complex network of narrative voices and apocalyptic tones is accurate or true, that it recaptures the intention of the one signed Derrida, even as author. ("Sounding the Unconscious" 34)

In light of these oscillations which disturb self-presence, the question is *how* to read *Glas*, a non-linear text whose disorienting effects appear a(es)thetically predicated upon the spatial logic of columns, evoking not only the vertical division of a page or table as in a newspaper column, but also, specifically, "the phallic columns of India" (*Glas* 2).

In *Glas*, Derrida plays the role of "columnist," not only in the sense of the journalist who provides miscellaneous commentary on people and events, but also through the production of a text that demonstrates the spatial effect of columns: vertical, tapering, cylindrical; in other words, an "object" that often serves as a monument. *Glas*, for example, is performative: it *does* what it says, a practice also illustrated by "Cartouches" in which the task for Derrida is, as Gregory Ulmer points out, "to mime in discourse a *visual* work" ("The Object" 93). In *Glas* the referents to be mimed are "at the beginning, the phallic columns of India, enormous formations, pillars, towers, larger at the base than at the top" (*Glas* 2–3). In effect, while *Glas* mimes the structuring properties of those columns it also evokes the "notches, excavations and openings" made in the columns drawing attention to those marks as writing that produces over time what might be called a *"collage effect"* (Ulmer, "The Object" 88):

Now at the outset – but as a setting out that already departed from itself – these columns were intact, unbreached [*inentamées*], smooth. And only later (*erst später*) are notches, excavations, openings (*Öffnungen und Aushöhlungen*) made in the columns, in the flank, if such can be said. These hollowings, holes, these lateral marks in depth would be like accidents coming over the phallic columns at first unperforated or apparently unperforatable. Images of gods (*Götterbilder*) were set, niched, inserted, embedded, driven in, tattooed on the columns. Just as these small caverns or lateral pockets on the flank of the phallus announced the small portable and hermetic Greek temples, so they broached/breached the model of the pagoda, not yet altogether a habitation and still distinguished by the separation between shell and kernel (*Schale und Kern*). A middle ground hard to determine between the column and the house, sculpture and architecture. (*Glas* 3)

A writing that produces "hollowings, holes [and] lateral marks in depth" is predicated upon the logic of a certain spacing that exceeds thetic referentiality. A writing in which "images of gods [are] set, niched, embedded, driven in, tattooed on the columns" escapes traditional mimesis because it follows the logic of encryption, a writing practice that *mimes the psychic process of cryptic incorporation*. As writing, it produces what can best be called the correspondence of the uncanny.

To whom does the uncanny address itself? Derrida's use of the word "enclave" earlier on (derived from *clavare*, f. *clavis*, key), is relevant here for it denotes "a foreign territory surrounded by one's own territory." This notion draws attention to the fact that the crypt marks a foreign place, prohibited, excluded within the "Self" where it implies the topography of an *other*. In *Glas*, this t(r)opography (of the other) paradoxically, is an *athetic* space: "a *middle* ground, hard to determine between the column and the house, sculpture and architecture" (*Glas* 3). The "middle ground" is "hard to determine" in part because of the crypt and all it implies. In fact, Derrida says of the crypt that it requires us to think about "a no-place or non-place within space" ("*Fors*" xxi). But the middle ground is also hard to determine because, as with the fantasy of cryptic incorporation, such a writing, written on the borderline between the outside and the inside, necessarily marks the place of (an uncanny) burial, which is what Derrida alludes to in "*Fors*": "we have recognized the crypt as (1) a certain organization of places [*lieux*] designed to *lead astray* and (2) a topographical arrangement made to keep (conserve-hidden) the *living dead*" (xxxvi). Thus, where it disturbs thetic referentiality, cryptomimesis also marks the place where Derrida diverges from the commonly accepted notion of otherness.

THE LAW OF ANOTHER GENERATION

I have said that cryptomimesis produces a kind of poetic language by playing with thetic referentiality. Such play disturbs what Kristeva refers to as "the specifically thetic function of *positing* the subject" ("Revolution" 109); it also subverts the denotative function – which Kristeva defines as "positing the object." I would argue that such disturbance undermines "the authority and the pertinence of the question 'What is …?'" ("This Strange Institution" 48). In short, to suspend the thetic relation is to confound (classical) distinctions between subject and object, or between self and other. But cryptomimesis also disturbs the notion of self-presence by bringing into the arena of subjectivity the notion of "the foreigner in the Self" which is how Derrida describes "not so much the commonly accepted otherness of the Unconscious," as put forward in Kristeva's argument, but a more "radical" otherness – that of "the heterocryptic ghost that *returns* from the Unconscious *of* the other, according to what might be called the law of *another generation*. The phenomenology of the ego or of the transcendental alter ego, governed by the principle of principles (the intuition of presence in self-presence), could only block the way" ("*Fors*" xxxi).

Cryptomimesis always concerns the other to whom Derrida entrusts his signature and whose ear will decide who signs, even to the extent of determining whether "the sex of the addresser" is male or female ("Roundtable on Autobiography" 52). But just as importantly, Derrida suggests that it is the figure of the mother who is "the ultimate addressee in the phantasm" (53). The speaker in the "Envois" evokes the maternal figure in relation to writing: "you can write only against your mother who bore within her, along with you, what she has borne you to write against her, your writing with which she would be large. And full, you will never get out of it" (150). Similarly, when Derrida says that Nietzsche "writes for" his mother, he draws attention to the figure of the one who makes utterance a possibility, as Kristeva suggests in her discussion of the thetic phase which is "a realm of positions" ("Revolution" 98), and of castration and the mirror stage in which "the mother occupies the place of alterity" (101). However, in Derrida's discussion of Nietzsche, it is the word "for" that again resonates uncannily, for the figure of the mother is implicit in the "ear of the other" and both evoke the notion of doubling. Here, in *this* work, the ear of the other who signs for Derrida is, shall we say *mine* but, like Nietzsche and the speaker in "Envois," I also "write for" and "against" my mother. And "my" ear, if it is "keen" enough, is the ear that Derrida says "says me to me and constitutes the *autos* of my autobiography" ("Roundtable on Autobiography 51). There's no getting out of it.

However, the ear that "says me to me" is also doubled, for, if Derrida, like Nietzsche, "writes *for*" his mother – that is, in the place of the other – the ear brings plurality into play in a way that the notion of "the commonly accepted otherness of the Unconscious" does not. I mention this here because it calls up another uncanny aspect of cryptomimesis which also, in a certain way, "says me to me." This "saying" in my engagement with Derrida's work involves the ear (whose? mine? Derrida's? yours?) and the reciprocal play between *auto* and *oto*.

We pass by way of the ear [says Derrida] – the ear involved in any autobiographical discourse that is still at the stage of hearing oneself speak.

(That is: I am telling myself a story, as Nietzsche said, here is the story that I am telling myself; and that means I hear myself speak). I speak myself to myself in a certain manner, and my ear is thus immediately plugged into my discourse and my writing. *But the necessity of passing onto and by way of the ear is not just this.* ("Roundtable on Autobiography" 49–50, emphasis mine)

It is "not just this" because of the many ears involved. The ear to whom I entrust my signature belongs not only to you (dear reader) even posthumously. To pass beyond the stage of merely "hearing myself" – to make possible the coming of the other – I have to undo a certain "closed structure" by admitting an uncanny doubleness, which is what Derrida suggests when, in "Otobiographies," he says, "your ear ... is *also* the ear of the other" (35). What comes undone in this admission is a certain model of presence which is founded on the experience of hearing oneself speak. Where the logic of self presence posits a certain interiority – the self-same (subject), shall we say – cryptomimesis undoes the hermeneutic circle by drawing upon the "foreigner in the Self" ("*Fors*" xxxi). By this I refer to what Derrida calls "the incorporated dead, [meaning that which one has not managed to assimilate through introjection and which] continues to lodge there *like something other* and to ventrilocate through the 'living'" ("Roundtable on Autobiography" 57–8, emphasis mine). While the space that cryptomimesis posits is cryptic, it becomes so only through the return of (the ghost of) the other which "ventri*locates*" the "I."

Inscribing the Wholly Other:
No Fixed Address

This is the end.

Jim Morrison, *The Doors*

While the analysis of the crypt has consequences for classical psychoanalysis, especially for the process of transference, the concept has equally far-reaching implications in terms of textual production. Recall what Derrida has said regarding the theory of the crypt and the ghost:

When it's a text that one is trying to decipher or decrypt using these concepts and these motifs, or when one is looking for a ghost or a crypt in a text, then things get still more difficult, or let us say more novel. I say a ghost *and* a crypt: actually the theory of the "ghost" is not exactly the theory of the "crypt." It's even more complicated. Although it's also connected to the crypt, the ghost is more precisely the effect of another's crypt in my unconscious. ("Roundtable on Autobiography" 59)

The "complications" entail what Derrida calls elsewhere "inventions of the same and of the other, of oneself as (of) the other" ("Psyche" 320). In short, cryptomimesis is not reducible to mere duplication. It involves the production of an uncanny imaginary space: of writing and reading *the other* writing and reading (the other). Derrida's remarks alert us to the possibility of a writing predicated upon the return of the (name of the) dead signing in the ear of the other. This is why Derrida says "I think one writes also *for* the dead" ("Roundtable on Autobiography" 53, emphasis mine). This structure is not limited to actual death but always to its possibility. The question of writing for the dead can be seen to be linked to what Alan Bass suggests is "the problematic of sending, particularly of *sending oneself* a letter, of creating an inheritance, a legacy" (xxviii). This is one way of understanding what Derrida means when he says that "every name is the name of someone dead, or of a living someone who it can do without" ("Roundtable on Autobiography 53). What lives on is the signature. Thus, when Derrida speaks of the revenant – the ghost that comes back from the crypt – we are drawn into thinking of writing that is predicated upon the return of the living-dead. Similarly, when Derrida remarks that the crypt is "the very condition of the whole enterprise, its element and its method," ("*Fors*" xiii) we hear Derrida's engagement with Heidegger. We also hear a general statement of cryptomimesis concerning its *condition*, its *element* and its *method*.[1] In short, the crypt is not to be read in terms of traditional allegoresis. Rather, it is to be considered, according to Derrida, in terms of a particular "engagement" which, through Derrida's use of the word in "*Fors*," we can understand as a contract with the dead.

This practice links the "first time" of invention to the anticipation of the future (other) coming as a ghost effect of the text. One can see this strategy in operation when Derrida, elaborating a model of Levinas's writing – a writing which Peggy Kamuf describes as "one that manages to inscribe or let be inscribed ... the altogether other" (403) – asks "How, then, does he write?" ("At This Very Moment" 412). With the use of an indeterminate pronoun "he," the question swings uncannily in the direction of *both* Levinas and Derrida. The needle also points in "my" direction and invites "me" to ask the question of "him" – "Derrida," the name that doubles for what haunts this work. "Derrida's" response to the question is equally uncanny because we can hear in it the provocation of Levinas's text signing in Derrida's ear as well as a spectral "voice" that amounts to the saying of the other which simultaneously countersigns "Derrida" *as* he writes. This consists in

inscribing the wholly other within the empire of the same, alter[ing] the same enough to absolve itself from itself. According to me [who?] that is his [whose? Levinas's? Derrida's?] answer, and that *de facto* answer, if one may say so, that response in deed, at work rather in the series of strategic negotiations, that response does not respond to a problem or a question;

it responds to the Other – and approaches [*aborde*] writing in enjoining itself to that for-the-Other. It is by starting from the Other that writing thus gives a place and forms an event. (412)

Responding "for-the-Other" is tied to the problematic of sending. The "strategic negotiation" of pronouns – me, his, one, it – provokes the movement of a specular structure that Derrida might call *revenance*, which implies the ghostly return of the *revenant,* and thus a coming back (to oneself).[2] As Alan Bass points out, *revenance* also carries the sense of *revenir à* – "to amount to" and "to fall to," as in an inheritance falling to someone – and *la venue*, which is the "coming," the "arrival" of something ("Glossary" xxix). Bass goes on to point out that *revenu* "also has the cognate English sense of revenue, or profit. In the general, or perhaps the exappropriative economy, one might say that 'revenue' consists of the attempt to bring back one's ghostly inheritance, which returns only to leave again, precisely because of the strings that are tied to it" (xxxix).

When, in *Specters of Marx*, Derrida remarks, "the *revenant* is going to come" (4), we can see not only how Derrida's *response* to Marx's *Communist Manifesto* constitutes a singular spectral effect of *that* text – what Derrida would call "signing but with a signature that countersigns" ("This Strange Institution" 66). We also see how Derrida's assertion can be said to describe the conditions of all textuality.

In *Specters of Marx*, Derrida remarks that "the dead can often be more powerful than the living" (48). If the dead shape the lives we are able to live, then they not only compel what we are able to read and to write but they also make it possible. Given that a revenant is both a legacy *and* a promise, this thinking of haunting always points towards a past *and* a future. Thinking of the phantom in these terms is, according to Derrida, "contrary to what good sense leads us to believe ... It is a thinking of the past, a legacy that can come only from that which has not yet arrived – from the *arrivant* itself" (196). In these terms, a text promises the *arrivant* itself, especially when it is unconscious or disavowed. This, too, describes the condition of textuality in general. It also draws attention to the matter of reading and writing for the dead. Even if we acknowledge the workings of the phantom in terms of texts and "subjects," how does one address oneself to a spectre? It is this structure that poses certain questions for "autobiography," but not only for reasons that have already been developed here. According to Derrida, the question deserves to be put another way:

Could one *address oneself in general* if already some ghost did not come back? If he [*sic*] loves justice at least, the "scholar" of the future, the "intellectual" of tomorrow should learn it and from the ghost. He should learn to live by learning not how to make conversation with the ghost but how to talk with him, with her, how to let them speak or how to give them back speech, even if it is in oneself, in the other, in the other in oneself: they are always *there*, specters, even if they do not exist, even if they are no longer, even if they are not yet. They give us to rethink the "there" as soon as we open our mouths. (*Specters* 176)

Arguably, Derrida has always concerned himself with the complications of what it takes to "learn to live." This refrain echoes throughout *Specters of Marx* directing us to the urgency behind Derrida's incessant questioning of textuality, subjectivity, truth, and fiction. To learn to live, we must learn how to talk "with" ghosts. Of course, it is the word *with* that illuminates the *workings* of what I have been calling cryptomimesis, which can be loosely defined as *ghost writing* in that, by drawing upon the theory of the phantom and the crypt, such writing problematizes notions of the subject, autobiography, and transference and, therefore, of textuality itself. In this instance, the word *with* produces a sense of simultaneity and doubleness. In cryptomimesis, talking with ghosts does not only mean being in conversation with them. It also means to use them instrumentally and, in turn, whether one knows it or *not*, to be used by them. In terms of textual production, cryptomimesis writes the other "even if they do not exist, even if they are no longer, even if they are not yet." And what makes possible the coming of the other in a work is, as cryptomimesis demonstrates, always a question of *haunting*, which is both a legacy and a promise to come.

Notes

THE FIRST PARTITION

1 Despite the revival of the Gothic, traces of the distinction made between "high" culture and popular culture remain entrenched in critical analyses of the genre. As Anne Williams points out in her discussion of the relationship between the Romantic poets and the Gothic, "by mid century, Romanticists were busy defending their favored poets against the Modernist assaults of the 1920s. As Sandra Gilbert and Susan Gubar have observed, the Modernist attitudes toward the nineteenth-century Romantic tradition barely concealed their hostile recognition of this literature as a culturally 'feminine' phenomenon – a celebration of emotion, intuition and the child" (5). And Stephen King is quick to point out that "in the more exalted circles of literary criticism," the label "horror novel" is "like the label 'pariah dog'" [*Danse Macabre* 166].

A more subtle but similar ambivalence occurs in the remarks made by Slavoj Žižek who, in his recent examination of the theoretical motifs of Jacques Lacan, proposes to read Lacan "with and through exemplary cases of contemporary mass culture," namely the works of Stephen King and others. It become clear that Žižek is aware of the bad press that Stephen King's work has received and takes pains to legitimize his attentions to King by placing him alongside Alfred Hitchcock, "about whom," says Žižek, reassuringly, "there is now general agreement that he was, after all, a '*serious artist*'" (vii, emphasis mine). Žižek also assures us that "the reader need not be uneasy" if "the book also mentions 'great' names like Shakespeare and Kafka," since, Žižek claims, they are to be read "strictly as kitsch authors, on the *same level* as ... King" (vii, emphasis mine). Although Žižek's use of quotation marks draws our attention to the fact that the distinction between "great" writers and "kitsch authors" is, in fact, an arbitrary one based on mechanisms of exclusion, his mention of his reader's "unease" is telling, especially since it is followed by the assurance that Shakespeare and Kafka will be read "on the same level" as King – that is, "strictly as kitsch authors" – an appellation that is double-edged since it implies that reading "on the same level" collapses the previous aesthetic hierarchies when, in fact, it subtly recapitulates them by recalling the opposition between "high" and "low" culture.

2 For example, see Gregory A. Waller's *The Living and the Undead: From Stoker's Dracula to Romero's Dawn of the Dead* in which Waller examines a group of texts – primarily novels and feature-length films – to formulate his (rather ambiguous) thesis that stories of the living-dead are "stories of the struggle for survival" of "the fittest of the living" (321). Although Waller never questions the term "living-dead," his study serves as an example of the proliferation of works focusing on Gothic horror which, curiously, has been done by those of a generation known as the "baby-boomers." Nina Auerbach's *Our Vampires, Ourselves* is another example of recent in-depth studies of horror. Auerbach reads Anglo-American cultural history – the assassinations of the Kennedys, the Vietnam War, Watergate, etc. – through changing perceptions of the living-dead in American popular culture, in particular, the vampire. In *The Monstrous-Feminine: Film, Feminism, Psychoanalysis*, Barbara Creed examines the representation of women in the role of the female vampire, suggesting that the female vampire is "abject because she disrupts identity and order" (61).

3 Žižek, *Looking Awry*. Albeit a dramatic statement, Žižek's assertion that the return of the living-dead is a fantasy of contemporary mass culture is not entirely on the mark, although the trope has become more prevalent, I think, because of film. The fantasy of the "living-dead" has been with us for much longer. According to Nicolas Abraham, the belief that the spirits of the dead can return to haunt the living is culturally integral and, he says, "exists either as an

accepted tenet or as a marginal conviction in all civilizations, ancient or modern" ("Notes on the Phantom," 171). Philippe Ariès also points out that after the boundaries between life and death became eroded in the art, literature, and medicine of the seventeenth and eighteenth centuries, "the living corpse became a constant theme, from baroque theater to the Gothic novel. But this strange theme did not remain confined to the world of the imagination. It invaded everyday life, and we meet it again in the form of the apparent death. In 1876 a doctor wrote that a "universal panic" had taken hold of people's minds at the idea of being buried alive, of waking up in the bottom of a grave" (396). Unless Žižek intends that the phrase "contemporary mass culture" be extended to include the nineteenth century, his remarks draw our attention to the *continuity* of the "fantasy" of the return of the living-dead as well as its transformations throughout time or, better yet, its tendency towards repetition.

Žižek's use of the term "fantasy" is important. Although he does provide a conceptual analysis of his use of the term, I wish to make clear that I am using it in the way described by Maria Torok in her 1959 essay, "Fantasy: An Attempt to Define Its Structure and Operation." In this essay Torok suggests that "if we claim that there is an underlying unconscious fantasy behind every human act, we strip fantasy of its specificity and operational value" (31). On the subject of fantasy, I agree with Torok who suggests that "even though the ego does participate in ... representation – which is why it can say, 'this is my fantasy' – it does not recognize itself directly as the active source of the fantasy. The ego has the impression rather of being the mere site of a strange and incomprehensible phenomenon. Since its reason for being as well as its aims are quite unknown, the representation gives rise to an impression of surprise, even gratuitousness. Something has happened outside the purview of the ego's concerns and suddenly *intruded* upon them in the form of a representation" (30).

4 Michel Foucault understands the Gothic novel in terms of the Enlightenment's "fear of darkened spaces, of the pall of gloom which prevents the full visibility of things, men and truths" ("The Eye of Power" 153). Structurally, Foucault sees the Gothic novel as an "imaginary space" which was antithetical to the political over-determination of the Revolution which wanted to "eliminate the shadowy areas of society, demolish the unlit chambers where arbitrary political acts, monarchical caprice, religious superstitions,

tyrannical and priestly plots, epidemics and the illusions of ignorance were fomented" (153).

Foucault's remarks also suggest that Gothic novels coming out of
the Revolutionary period can be read in psychoanalytic terms since,
he says, they "develop a whole fantasy-world of stone walls, darkness, hideouts and dungeons which harbour, in significant complic-
ity, brigands and aristocrats, monks and traitors" (154). While
Foucault and Jameson focus attention upon Gothic fiction in general terms of psychoanalysis, politics, and class, critics such as
Michelle A. Massé and Anne Williams argue specifically for feminist
readings of Gothic fiction. Massé claims that works such as Anne
Radcliffe's *The Mysteries of Udolpho* and Charlotte Perkins
Gilman's *The Yellow Wallpaper* concern themselves with "the prohibition of female autonomy" (681) and can thus be read in psychoanalytic terms of "transgression, regression, repetition," which she
calls "the stuff of analysis itself and of the Gothic" (683). Like
Massé, Williams argues for a "female Gothic," which she claims
"expresses the terror and rage that women experience within patri-
archal social arrangements, especially marriage" (136).

5 I am referring to the works of Nicolas Abraham and Maria Torok,
specifically *The Wolf Man's Magic Word* and *The Shell and the
Kernel*.

6 It is important to mention that Derrida's Gothic inclinations have
not been totally ignored although where the Gothic *is* mentioned, its
name is used in the pejorative. Geoffrey Hartman broaches the significance of haunting in Derrida's work when he remarks that
"Derrida turns even psychoanalysis into a modern Gothic affair" (xviii).
Hartman draws back, however, from further development of this
thought since he wants "to avoid the charge of mystification" (xix),
asserting that the issues of "nonbeing and death need not be left to
religious mysticism or the modern Gothic or science fiction" (xviii).
Hartman's remarks suggest that religious mysticism, the modern
Gothic, and science fiction are not only vaguely analogous but they
also share some fundamentally *improper* peculiarity that renders
them inappropriate to a discussion of Derrida's work. Hartman's
recognition of the significance of haunting in Derrida's work, however, is implicit in his rhetorical question regarding the nature of
Derrida's engagement with psychoanalysis: "Does [psychoanalysis]
not repeople the mind with dead persons and dread voices" (xviii)?
Likewise, in drawing an analogy between the desire on the part of

psychoanalysis, which takes the form of "a quest for totality" (xviii), and philosophy's "wish for total intelligibility" (xvii), Hartman implies that Derrida sees psychoanalysis as a discourse taken up with hauntings and the return of the dead, and that he also considers Western metaphysics to be a haunted structure wherein writing appears, as Derrida says elsewhere, as a "ghost-effect."

7 "Live burial" is also an appropriate term to describe Abraham and Torok's concept of the crypt: once constituted during unsuccessful mourning, it then holds or houses the incorporated dead who continues to lodge there as an "other" – a living-dead – to ventriloquize the living.

8 See also Ernest Baker's discussion of Byron who had read Harriet Lee's *Kruitzner*. Byron's play was modelled on the story in which the count's father had cursed his degenerate son who in turn feels himself involved in a maze where he "can only flutter/Like the poor fly, but break it not." Baker finds that fate is intrinsic to the Gothic: "it is the Gothic idea of ineluctable fate impelling to crime, for which the wrongdoer feels shame and remorse, yet knows that it is useless to struggle against the decree: his is predestined to evil" (184). This predestination to evil is certainly true of Walpole's *The Castle of Otranto*.

9 Maud Mannoni's *Le Premier rendez-vouz avec le psychoanalyste*, qtd. in Gunn, *Psychoanalysis and Fiction*, 77.

10 Although some of the texts to which I will refer are transcripts from both interviews and lectures, I do not intend to discriminate between text and transcript since my concern is with developing the notion of cryptomimesis.

11 See Derrida, *The Post Card*, 148–52. Riddel is referring to the "scene" referred to in the post card dated 20 June 1978 which Riddel says "is an address, in one or more of its senses, of an 'I' to a 'you' and recounts the 'return' to Zurich of the sender who has been met at the airport by someone named 'Hillis,' an otherwise anonymous friend who transports the writer to a nearby cemetery where the two pass some time walking about in conversation, happening upon Joyce's tomb and speaking, to quote the card, 'I believe, about Poe and Yale, all that'" (Riddel, 17–18).

12 Esther Rashkin's study of narrative, like Derrida's analysis of Marx, draws upon the clinical writings of Nicolas Abraham and Maria Torok – in particular their discussion of secrets, theories of the phantom, the crypt, anasemia, incorporation, and cryptonymy.

Whereas Rashkin's study of narrative takes up "the haunting effects of family secrets" (3), Derrida's work invokes the figure of the spectre/phantom as an effect of transgenerational and cultural haunting in terms of writing and subjectivity. Although Rashkin's study of the relationship between haunting and narrative is predicated upon the issue of interpersonal familial haunting and thus differs from Derrida's sense that haunting is a phenomenon affecting entire generations, both focus their discussion of phantoms and haunting in *texts* and *writing*. For example, Rashkin claims that Joseph Conrad's *The Secret Sharer* functions as an "allegory of the phantom structure" (9), a remark which is based upon her sense that the "first-person account [of the captain]... emerges as a narrative driven by the phantom [an unspeakable secret] lodged within him, and [thus] as an implicit commentary on the potential link between phantomatic secret, the generative force of narrative, and the formation of allegory in literature (9).

13 See, for example, "Berenicë: A Tale," "Morella," "The Fall of the House of Usher," "The Black Cat," and "The Tell-Tale Heart," to name but a few of Poe's stories that deal with the theme of burial and return from the dead.

14 This notion of trauma being excluded is maintained throughout Abraham and Torok's work, especially in *The Shell and the Kernel* in which they argue that repression also acts upon words themselves. See also Nicholas T. Rand's introduction to this work entitled, "Renewals of Psychoanalysis."

15 See Derrida's essay "At This Very Moment in This Work Here I Am," which poses certain questions of the writings of Emmanuel Levinas (Kamuf, *Derrida Reader*, 405–39).

16 Although I have been referring specifically to Derrida's use of certain tropes and topoi, I mean, of course, to draw attention to the affinity between Derrida's concerns with language/writing and that of the Gothic. See Eve Kosofsky Sedgwick's *The Coherence of Gothic Conventions* in which she discusses language/writing in terms of the genre's structural and thematic preoccupation with the link between writing and dream, with the "unspeakable" and with "irrevocable doubleness." Sedgwick claims, for example, that "written language 'is' Gothic" (63), especially correspondence. She says "'correspondence' is distinguished from direct communication, which is seen as impossible; instead it moves by a relation of counterparts and doubles, and is subject to dangerous distortions and interferences" (40).

In *Art of Darkness: A Poetics of Gothic*, Anne Williams draws attention to similar concerns with language and writing when she argues
that "Gothic conventions ... imply a fascination with the problem of
language, with possible fissures in the system of the Symbolic as a
whole. Most – perhaps *all* – Gothic conventions express some anxiety about 'meaning.' In Gothic, fragments of language often serve
ambiguously to further the plot – in letters (lost, stolen, buried); in
mysterious warnings, prophecies, oaths, and curses; in lost wills and
lost marriage lines. Such fragments may be misinterepreted (often
because they are removed from the original context), and frequently
deceive or betray the interpreter" (67). Williams goes on to say that
"in Gothic, language is multifarious, duplicitous, and paradoxical"
(67). It seems to me that Derrida's concern with language is remark-
ably similar to those put forward by Sedgwick and Williams.

17 See for example Nina Auerbach's *Our Vampires, Ourselves* in which
she examines five film adaptations of *Dracula* (between 1931 and
1992) in relation to changing ideologies of power. Auerbach questions, for example, the links between the anxieties of the Persian
Gulf War and those of Anne Rice's Lestat and his contemporaries.
Auerbach also claims that "history and horror are inseparable"
demonstrating her point in a discussion of the links between George
Romero's *Night of the Living Dead* (1968) and the war in Vietnam:
"In many movies, folklore vampires were replacing glamorized
Hammer corpses; Romero's *Night of the Living Dead* is overrun
with these awkward, festering, feasting revenants. Graphic footage
of the war in Vietnam, the assassinations and rumblings of civil war
at home, had made corpses revert to the rot and dread they had
embodied before the so-called enlightenment of the eighteenth
century, when they gained the potential to become uplifting icons"
(note 59, 214). See also Underwood and Miller, *Bare Bones*, in
which Stephen King links Watergate with *Salem's Lot*: "I know that,
for instance, in my novel *Salem's Lot*, the thing that really scared me
was not vampires, but the town in the daytime, the town that was
empty, knowing that there were things in closets, that there were
people tucked under beds, under the concrete pilings of all those
trailers. And all the time I was writing that, the Watergate hearings
were pouring out of the TV. There were people saying 'at that point
in time.' They were saying, 'I can't recall.' There was money show-
ing up in bags. Howard Baker kept asking, 'What I want to know
is, what did you know and when did you know it?' That line haunts

me, it stays in my mind. It may be *the* classic line of the twentieth century" (5).

18 In *The Wolf Man's Magic Word: A Cryptonymy*, Abraham and Torok discuss the analysis of Freud's most well-known analysand – the Wolf Man – in terms of incorporation versus introjection, developing the notion of the crypt and cryptonymy to articulate their reinterpretation of the notion of fantasy in which the Self is "haunted" by the "ghost" of the "living-dead" that "comes haunting out of the Unconscious of the other" yet which resides as an "inhabitant of the crypt within the Self."

   It is important to make a distinction here between Jacques Lacan's conception of the signifying chain and the concept of cryptonymy (since the work of Abraham and Torok – because it concerns itself with elaborating language as a system of expressive traces – seems to have influenced Derrida's deconstructive methods and also his writing practice).

   Lacan's understanding of the individual as subject to an indelible lack of being is, according to Nicholas Rand, "formulated in linguistic terms as the irreducible separation or barrier between a progressive chain of interlocking signifiers and stable meanings (i.e. signifieds)" (*Wolf Man's* lx). Rand points out that the distinction between Lacan's concept and that of Abraham and Torok is a crucial one: "While cryptonymic analysis acknowledges the mobility of the signifying chain, it operates by studying the *nature of the barrier* that serves to separate the chain of signifiers from a potential signified" (lx, emphasis mine). Thus it is the bar or the barrier itself that becomes the subject of inquiry.

19 Although I agree with Rashkin's contention that the theory of the phantom and haunting lends itself to textual analysis, I find her assertion that "not all texts have phantoms" (10) to be problematic because her assertion marks a division between texts which reveal "secrets" and those that do not (presumably those that do not harbour an unspeakable secret are transparent). Similarly, because her concept of "text" seems confined to the book and to so-called fiction (in the same way that writing is reduced to the empirical), her remarks have the effect of repressing the notion that textuality extends to culture, ideology, the family, and even the so-called subject, all of which might be understood in terms of transgenerational haunting and spectral effects.

20 The dream, as Freud described it, provides a model with which to think through the cross-currents flowing through Derrida's writing since, according to Freud, "a dream is a picture puzzle," but one which is multiply-determined through condensation and displacement. As Derrida suggests, dream writing, like the rebus, requires a different kind of reading since it is "not an inscribed image but a figurative script" ("Freud and the Scene of Writing" 218). That the rebus requires a different kind of reading can be heard in Freud's assertion that "if we attempted to read these characters according to their pictorial value instead of according to their symbolic relation, we should clearly be led into error" since, "dream-thoughts and the dream-content [the latent and the manifest] are presented to us like two versions of the same subject-matter in two different languages. Or, more properly, the dream-content seems like a transcript of the dream-thoughts into another mode of expression, whose characters and syntactic laws it is our business to discover by comparing the original and the translation" (*Interpretation of Dreams*, 381–2). Freud's insistence that the rebus demands another kind of reading functions as a rebuttal to what he describes as his "predecessors in the field of dream-interpretation [who] have made the mistake of treating the rebus as a pictorial composition" and, reading it thus, assert that it is "non-sensical and worthless" (382). Freud's remarks can also be understood as a statement of aesthetics or, better yet, a poetics. As Freud says, "obviously we can only form a proper judgment of the rebus if we put aside criticisms such as these of the whole composition and its parts and if, instead, we try to replace each separate element by a syllable or word that can be presented by that element in some way or another. The words which are put together in this way are no longer nonsensical but may form *a poetical phrase of the greatest beauty and significance*" (382, emphasis mine).

THE RETURN OF THE LIVING DEAD

1 See also Alan Bass's translation of this passage of "Signature Event Context" in Kamuf, *A Derrida Reader*, 97.
2 See Gregory Ulmer's discussion of decomposition in terms of the mouth and orality in *Applied Grammatology* (56–63).
3 This notion of the ego as the mask of the phantom (other) offers a reversal of Freud's metapsychological formula in "Mourning and

Melancholia," which conceives the ego in the guise of the object. What ensues through incorporation, is, instead, a "cryptofantasy" determined by an "endocryptic" identification that is both imaginary and *secret*.

4 Quoted by Gayatri Spivak in the Translator's Preface to *Of Grammatology*, xxiii.

5 It is interesting that Derrida, who can be counted upon to employ semantically double-edged words, uses the term "host" since it refers not only to a "large number" but it also carries with it the notion of "parasite."

6 Right now I am tempted to leave in place a typographical error which I have just made in entering the above quotation in order to "multiply the example" that I have just given. Instead of typing "I am singing a death," as is written in "Envois," I (?) write "I am *signing* a death." Then, in reading what I have placed in parenthesis, I notice that I have written, in the first instance, "I am singing a *dead*!"

MAKING A CONTRACT WITH THE DEAD

1 I am indebted to Lorraine Weir for this thought.

2 According to Bakhtin, heteroglossia is the base condition of language in that "all utterances are heteroglot" (428). Similarly, hybridization refers to the potential of language to belong "simultaneously to two or more systems" within "a single concrete utterance" (429).

3 See Jane Gallop's discussion of imagoes in *Reading Lacan* (60–5), in which she says, "the imaginary [Lacan's] is made up of *imagoes*."

4 Thanks to Michael Zeitlin who also points out that "pet" indicates "favourite" in the jocular sense of a thing or person particularly disliked ("pet peeve" or "pet aversion").

5 In *Jack the Ripper: "Light-Hearted Friend,"* Richard Wallace demonstrates in detail how anagrammatic readings of texts suggest the encoding of incorporated material. Through a reading of the works of Charles Dodgson (better known as Lewis Carroll, author of *Alice in Wonderland*), Wallace contends that Carroll, a don at Oxford University, appears not only to have suffered a psychotic break but also to have moved "from performing rather benign antisocial acts in secret to being a full-blown psychopathic killer [otherwise known as Jack the Ripper]." Wallace suggests that "the means for Dodgson's encoding was a word game in which he is known to have excelled –

anagrams" (37). Although Wallace's analysis of Charles Dodgson's works is detailed, a brief excerpt will demonstrate the extent to which this reader was compelled to respond:

[Dodgson's] first anagrams were simple. For example, in *Sylvie and Bruno*, Dodgson toys with his readers when he has the fairy Bruno made the word *evil* out of *live* just by "twiddling" his eyes. In later works, more complex anagrams emerge with much angrier and sexually explicit themes, such as the "Marchioness of Mock Turtles," which can become "O fuck mother's incest morals." [Wallace asks us to] consider the opening verse to "Jabberwocky," thought to be the greatest piece of nonsense literature in the English language ... [arguing that if] based on punctuation we treat the verse as three anagrams – the first two lines together and the last two separately – we have a totally different poem, which reflects Dodgson's struggles and predicts the nature of the murders:

But I beat my glands til,
With hand-sword I slay the evil gender.
A slimey theme; borror gloves,
And masturbate the hog more!

6 This term is used by Derrida in *Glas* when speaking of Genet, who "has often feigned to define the 'magnifying' operation of his writing by the act of nomination. The allegation seems frequent enough that we could suspect it of a certain refrain-effect." Derrida's question draws attention to how the imposition of a recurring phrase or line in a song also suggests the notion of repression, restraint, abstention, and thus, curbing (5).

THE QUESTION OF THE TOMB

1 Derrida, "A 'Madness' Must Watch Over Thinking," 349.
2 Derrida, "The Theater of Cruelty," 232.
3 Derrida, *Glas*, 1.
4 Derrida, "Structure, Sign and Play," 292.
5 Kamuf, *Derrida Reader*, 315. She is speaking of the Editions Galilée edition of *Glas* when she mentions that the work is comprised of 283 pages.
6 Derrida, *Glas*, 1, 262.
7 Derrida, "Signature Event Context," 90.

8 Kamuf, *Derrida Reader,* 315.

9 Stoker, *Dracula,* 302–3.

10 Derrida "Structure, Sign and Play," 293.

11 Ibid., 293.

12 Derrida, *Glas,* 6.

13 In Auerbach, *Our Vampires,* 23.

14 Ibid., 23.

15 Ibid., 23.

16 Georges Bataille, *Erotism: Death and Sensuality,* 55–8.

17 Kristeva, *Powers of Horror,* 3.

18 Derrida, "The Theater of Cruelty," 243.

19 Derrida, *Glas,* 4.

20 Stoker, *Dracula,* 303.

21 Ibid., 123.

22 Ibid., 301–2.

23 Yeats, "The Second Coming," 91

24 Quoted in Gregory Ulmer, "The Object of Post-Criticism," 100.

25 Arthur Conan Doyle, "The Parasite," (1894).

26 Derrida, "Structure, Sign, and Play," *Writing and Difference,* 292.

27 Ibid., 292.

28 Anne Rice, *The Vampire Lestat,* 275.

29 See Derrida, "Signature Event Context" in which he demonstrates "why a context is never absolutely determinable" or "in what way its determination is never certain or saturated" (84).

30 Kristeva's remarks draw attention to the proliferation of contexts, namely myth, folk tale, religion, psychoanalysis, and now deconstruction, in which the return of the living-dead is a central concern. Why do the dead return from the grave? Žižek points out that "the answer offered by Lacan is the same as that found in popular culture: *because they were not properly buried*" (23). Montague Summers has assembled an exhaustive collection of literary and anecdotal material tracing the return of the dead from the grave, including the vampire and the revenant, as they appear throughout ancient Greece and Rome, England, Ireland, Hungary, Czechoslovakia, and Modern Greece, Russia, Romania, and Bulgaria. From Virgil onwards, there seems to be a consensus that "a person who has not received decent rites of burial and fitting exsequies" (31) would return to demand some form of recompense from the living. This is, of course, prime material for the Gothic.

AN ART OF CHICANERY

1 I do not confine my understanding of "Gothic" to either the novel or to fiction (even though I use these distinctions at certain times), but take as a point of departure an observation made by Anne Williams that the so-called Gothic emerges out of a *poetic* tradition. See Anne Williams's *Art of Darkness*. Williams claims about this tradition that

> The reader searching for "Gothic" in a novel (as well as "the novel" in Gothic) realizes that Walpole's inspiration [for the *Castle of Otranto*] derives not only from a few scenes in Smollett and Richardson, but also from a farrago of poetry, drama, architecture, painting, landscape gardening, and antiquarian enthusiasm for the medieval (or rather for eighteenth-century fantasies of those "Dark Ages") ... Although earlier critics insisted on the importance of foreign – especially German – imports, many scenes and episodes in canonical literature belong to a kind of quasi-"Gothic" tradition that may be traced from *Beowulf* (the landscape of Grendel's mere) through several episodes of *The Faerie Queene*, certain scenes from Shakespeare, much of Jacobean drama, to Milton's "Il Penseroso," verse by Anne Finch, and Pope's *Eloisa to Abelard*. By the 1740s, the works of the "Graveyard School" suggest that what we now called "Gothic" appeared to be quintessentially "poetic." (13)

Similarly, the distinction made between the Gothic "romance" and the realist novel, and even between branches of the Gothic, for example, enact the (aesthetic) division that philosophy makes to partition one kind of writing from another, a gesture which also functions to detach (and exalt) "literature" from criticism.

Anne Williams makes the point that even though the word "Gothic" today "seems most appropriately followed by the word "novel" (2) – an indication that we have been encouraged, says Williams, to conflate "prose fiction" and "novel" – there has been "no easy way to distinguish between early Gothic and several texts we count among the masterpieces of Romantic poetry" (3). Williams also draws attention to the fact that criticism has not only been loath to admit any connection between Gothic prose and Romantic poetry – citing as examples of the high Romantics' affinity for Gothic,

Williams includes Coleridge's "Mystery Poems," Keats's "Belle Dame sans Merci," "Lamia," and "The Eve of St. Agnes," Shelley's *Alastor*, Wordsworth's "Lucy" lyrics, and the early "Salisbury Plain" – all these, she suggests are "replete with Gothic paraphernalia: fatal women, haunted castles, bleeding corpses, and mysterious warnings" (3–4) – but criticism has, with the exception of a few apologists actively disavowed any (familial?) ties. Citing as an example of this aesthetic division Robert D. Hume's influential essay "Gothic versus Romantic: A Re-evaluation of the Gothic Novel" (1969), Williams quotes Hume as saying, "the Gothic literary endeavor is not that of the transcendent romantic imagination; rather, in Coleridge's terms, Gothic writers are working with fancy, which is bound to the 'fixities and definites' of the rational world" (6).

It is clear that Williams considers herself one of the apologists for Gothic, especially where the Romanticist's definition of the genre, as one that is both "immanent and material" coincides with the view that designates the romance as "Realism's 'other'" (7). Both these views, suggests Williams, are aligned with the denigration of the female, or "woman" as she is traditionally represented in Western culture: the negation of the first term of any hierarchical opposition: real/imaginary, experience/dream, rational/irrational, transcendence/immanence, conscious/unconscious. From this perspective, "woman" is physical, non-transcendental and, as such, represents a threat to logic, reason, and truth, even though she can be a symbol of truth.

2 Deleuze, *The Fold* (qtd. in Blaser, *The Holy Forest*, 370).

3 See also Mark Taylor who points out what is at stake in thinking the not: "thought cannot think without thinking not, [and] the Western ontological tradition has, in effect, been in an extended effort not to think not"(1). What I am calling Derrida's poetics is a way of circumventing the law – the imperative "not to think not" – while maintaining it in all its contradictions.

4 One example of nostalgia for the loss of meaning appears in "Filling in the Millennium" by Kent Nussey: "The meaning muscle has become nearly vestigial, a generally useless little appendage that we fall back on only when cornered, only in the face of larger public catastrophes that require meaning to keep the social process ongoing. In our private lives, we have long since given up on meaning. If we looked for it in our various domestic disasters, in our lost children and lost jobs, our botched elections and divorces, we would soon give way to an inexorable despair that would render us wholly

dysfunctional. The death of meaning has become a cruel necessity; it seems that to accept its loss is the only way to get one's self up each day for another shift in the mines, another hack at the endless procurement of monies, which is the final test of the individual's authenticity in this culture" (24).

5 Maurice Blanchot, "The End of Philosophy," in Derrida, *Specters of Marx*, 36.

6 See also Romans 8:9; I Corinthians 3:16; and John 20:22.

7 The term "Supreme Being" is taken from the translation of Stirner and appears in Derrida's *Specters of Marx*, in a footnote on page 191. The term "highest essence" appears in Max Stirner's *The Ego and Its Own*.

8 Stirner seems aware of the contentiousness of periodization. An editorial footnote to Stirner's remarks states, "'Romanticism [*Romantik*]' refers to a late eighteenth and early nineteenth century movement of writers and artists (typically contrasted with the classicism of Goethe and Schiller). Its characterization and categorization are fiercely contested ... Here Stirner seems concerned to point out that, in reacting against the fragmentation and disenchantment of the modern world, the Romantics – including E.T.A. Hoffman (1776–1822), Jacob Grimm (1785–1863), and his brother Wilhelm Grimm (1786–1859) – rediscovered an interest in folk songs, folklaw, and fairy tales. In this context Stirner links the Romantic movement with the fashionable spiritual and scientific interest in magnetism, somnambulism, and Mesmerism" (footnote 333).

One might speculate on the similarities between our current culture's concerns with new-age spiritualism and psychic phenomena and late eighteenth- and early nineteenth-century Romanticism, especially since the current *fin de siècle*/millennium has been described in secular terms. What returns to haunt? Does the current revival of Gothic themes and tropes, especially the return of the dead from the grave, suggest a nostalgic desire for a return to univocal meaning in what has been described as a secular age? Or, as Derrida's writing suggests, do the tropes and topoi of the Gothic show us that, rather than being unique to the Gothic, haunting, mourning, and revenance are integral components of subjectivity, language, and thought, thus comprising social and cultural reality?

9 Although still concerned with the return of the dead from the grave or, the so-called living dead, current works in popular culture differ from earlier representations of the return of the living dead in more

than one important aspect. On the one hand, Polidori's Lord Ruthven in *The Vampyre*, Le Fanu's Carmilla, and Stoker's Dracula are all represented not only as individuals who are connected to the aristocracy and who have rank and power but also as embodiments of pure evil, who must also be destroyed at any cost. On the other hand, current manifestations of the living-dead in fiction and film are more sympathetic to the plight of the "monster," while they are also sustained by a profound nostalgia! Coppola's Dracula, for example, is shown not as an arch fiend but rather as a creature who has "lived" in mourning for centuries, haunted by the death of his wife who was manipulated into suicide by the Count's political enemies who gave her a false report of his death on the battlefield. When he learns of his wife's death, Vlad Tepes a proud man, is overcome by grief and is damned when he renounces God. (While some critics suggest that Bram Stoker modelled his Count on Vlad Tepes, also known as Vlad the Impaler, a historical figure, Coppola's version makes them one and the same.) Dracula's hopes are rekindled, however, when Jonathan Harker shows up bearing the photographic image of his new wife, Mina Harker, who just might be the nineteenth-century reincarnation of the Count's beloved. Similarly, Anne Rice's postmodern vampire, Louis, is tormented by his "nature" as the need to kill fills him with self-loathing and he confines himself, whenever possible, to killing either "strangers," or animals. Louis also concerns himself with the moral and ethical consequences of his actions, expressing sentiments that were unimaginable in previous representations of the vampire. For example, Louis profoundly regrets that Lestat, his mentor, did not give him a choice but made him start by killing a person rather than an animal. Louis asserts that even though the decision is an aesthetic one, it is also moral since, as he assures his interlocutor, "'all aesthetic decisions are moral, really'" (78). In contrast to the ruthlessness of his predecessors, Louis agonizes not only over questions of the existence of God and of evil but also of his own *being*. In his "interview," he tells of walking the streets before dawn relentlessly questioning himself, "'Am I damned? Am I from the devil? Is my very nature that of a devil? I was asking myself over and over. And if it is, why then do I revolt against it? ... What have I become in becoming a vampire? Where am I to go?'" (79).

10 See, for example, Doris Lessing's *Prisons We Choose to Live Inside* in which she suggests "it is the heritage of the structure of Christian

thought in us that we should study" (31). Lessing makes this assertion based upon her perception that the notion of redemption prevails in Communist and socialist thought as a legacy of the "structure of Christian thinking" (32).

11 "*Fors*" refers the reader to the premises of *The Wolf Man's Magic Word* which Derrida finds analogous to deconstruction: "There is an extraordinary continuity, a striking coherence between the 1961 program and all the *anasemic* research of the later work. From the very first page of the 1961 manuscript, in the first paragraph ('The Text of the Symbol') of the first chapter ('Psychoanalysis and Transphenomenology of the Symbol'), one recognizes *The Magic Word's* milieu" (xxix).

INSCRIBING THE WHOLLY OTHER

1 See Derrida's discussion of the crypt in "*Fors.*" This essay seems to be, in part, a response to Heidegger's "Letter on Humanism." In that essay, Heidegger speaks of the history of Being which, he says, "sustains and defines every *condition et situation humaine*" (Heidegger, "Letter" 194). Here, Heidegger also asserts that "we must free ourselves from the technical interpretation of thinking," (194) and he is careful to point out that thinking is not logic, ethics, or physics – systems of thought that arose, says Heidegger, "when original thinking comes to an end" (195). Heidegger goes on to say that "thinking comes to an end when it slips out of its element. The element is what enables thinking to be a thinking" (196). What I am interested in is Derrida's use of the terms "condition," and "element." It suggests a certain "engagement" – a word used by Derrida when speaking of the crypt and by Heidegger when speaking of thinking as "*l'engagement par l'Être pour l'Être* [engagement by Being for Being]" – with Heidegger's thought that amounts to the uncanny sound of Heidegger's name *signing* in "Derrida's" ear, where that organ might be thought of as a crypt. (The verb *to engage* not only means "to bind (by contract or promise)," "to fasten," or "to pledge oneself (to do)" but also "to undertake," where that verb can also suggest an obligation to [tracing the works of] the dead.)

2 See Alan Bass, "Glossary," xxix.

Bibliography

Abraham, Nicolas. *Rhythms: On the Work, Translation and Psychoanalysis*. Translated by Benjamin Thigpen and Nicholas T. Rand. Stanford: Stanford University Press, 1995.

– "The Intermission of 'Truth.'" In Abraham and Torok, *The Shell and the Kernel*, 187–90.

– "The Shell and the Kernel: The Scope and Originality of Freudian Psychoanalysis." In Abraham and Torok, *The Shell and the Kernel*, 79–98.

– "Notes on the Phantom: A Complement to Freud's Metapsychology." In Abraham and Torok, *The Shell and the Kernel*, 171–76.

Abraham, Nicolas, and Maria Torok. "'The Lost Object–Me': Notes on Endocryptic Identification." In Abraham and Torok, *The Shell and the Kernel*, 139–56.

– "Mourning *or* Melancholia: Introjection *versus* Incorporation." In *The Shell and the Kernel*, 125–38.

– "The Sandman Looks at 'The Uncanny.'" In *Speculations After Freud: Psychoanalysis, Philosophy and Culture*. Edited by Sonu Shamdasani and Michael Münchow, 185–203. New York: Routledge, 1994.

– *The Shell and The Kernel: Renewals of Psychoanalysis*. Vol. 1. Translated and edited by Nicholas T. Rand. Chicago: University of Chicago Press, 1994.

– "The Topography of Reality: Sketching a Metaphychology of Secrets." In Abraham and Torok, *The Shell and the Kernel*, 157–61.

– *The Wolf Man's Magic Word: A Cryptonymy.* Translated by Nicholas Rand. Minneapolis: University of Minnesota Press, 1986.

Ariès, Phillipe. *The Hour of Our Death.* Translated by Helen Weaver. New York: Knopf, 1981.

Attridge, Derek. "Derrida and the Questioning of Literature." Introduction to Derrida, *Acts of Literature*, 1–29. New York: Routledge, 1992.

Auerbach, Nina. *Our Vampires, Ourselves.* Chicago: University of Chicago Press, 1995.

Bahti, Timothy, and Richard Klein. Introduction to "The Ghost of Theology: Readings of Kant and Hegel." *Diacritics* 11, no. 2 (Summer 1981): 1.

Baker, Ernest A. *The Novel of Sentiment and the Gothic Romance.* Vol. 5 of *The History of the English Novel.* New York: Barnes and Noble, 1957.

Bakhtin, M.M. "Discourse in the Novel." *The Dialogic Imagination.* Translated by Caryl Emerson and Michael Hopkins. Edited by Michael Holquist, 258–422. Austin: University of Texas Press, 1981.

Barthes, Roland. "The Death of the Author." *Image, Music, Text.* Translated by Stephen Heath, 142–48. New York: Hill and Wang, 1977.

Bass, Alan. "Glossary." In Derrida, *The Post Card: From Socrates to Freud and Beyond.*

Bataille, Georges. *Erotism: Death and Sensuality.* Translated by Mary Dalwood. San Francisco: City Lights Books, 1986.

Benjamin, Walter. "The Task of the Translator." *Illuminations.* Translated by Harry Zohn, edited by Hannah Arendt, 69–82. New York: Schocken, 1968.

Blanchot, Maurice. "Literature and the Right to Death." *The Gaze of Orpheus.* Translated by Lydia Davis. Barrytown, N.Y.: Station Hill, 1981.

Blaser, Robin. *The Holy Forest.* Toronto: Coach House Press, 1993.

Bracken, Christopher. "White Gift: The Potlatch and the Rhetoric of Canadian Colonialism, 1868–1936." Ph.D. Dissertation. University of British Columbia, 1996.

Bronfen, Elisabeth. *Over Her Dead Body: Death, Femininity and the Aesthetic.* New York: Routledge, 1992.

Buck-Morss, Susan. *The Dialectics of Seeing: Walter Benjamin and the Arcades Project.* Cambridge: MIT Press, 1989.

Burnham, Clint. *The Jamesonian Unconscious: The Aesthetics of Marxist Theory.* Durham: Duke University Press, 1995.

Butler, Judith. *Gender Trouble: Feminism and the Subversion of Identity.* New York: Routledge, 1990.

Carroll, Nöel. *The Philosophy of Horror or, Paradoxes of the Heart.* New York: Routledge, 1990.

Cixous, Hélène. *Three Steps on the Ladder of Writing.* New York: Columbia University Press, 1993.

– "Sorties." In *The Newly Born Woman,* by Hélène Cixous and Catherine Clément. Translated by Betsy Wing. Vol. 24 of *Theory and History of Literature.* Minneapolis: University of Minnesota Press, 1986.

Creed, Barbara. *The Monstrous-Feminine: Film, Feminism, Psychoanalysis.* New York: Routledge, 1993.

De Man, Paul. *Allegories of Reading: Figural Language in Rousseau, Nietzsche, Rilke, and Proust.* New Haven: Yale University Press, 1979.

– "The Dead End of Formalist Criticism." *Blindness and Insight: Essays in the Rhetoric of Contemporary Criticism.* 2d ed. Minneapolis: University of Minnesota Press, 1983.

Deleuze, Gilles, and Félix Guattari. *A Thousand Plateaus: Capitalism and Schizophrenia.* Translated by Brian Massumi. Minneapolis: University of Minnesota Press, 1987.

Derrida, Jacques. "A 'Madness' Must Watch Over Thinking." In *Points: Interviews, 1974–1994.* Translated by Peggy Kamuf, edited by Elisabeth Weber, 339–64. Stanford: Stanford University Press, 1995.

– *Acts of Literature.* Edited by Derek Attridge, translated by Geoffrey Bennington and Rachel Bowlby. New York: Routledge, 1992.

– *Aporias.* Translated by Thomas Dutoit. Stanford: Stanford University Press, 1993.

– "Art of *Memoires.*" In *Memoires for Paul de Man,* 45–88.

– "At This Very Moment in This Work Here I Am." Translated by Ruben Berezdivin. In Peggy Kamuf, ed., *A Derrida Reader,* 403–39.

– "Before the Law." Translated by Avital Ronell and Christine Roulston. In *Acts of Literature,* 181–220.

– "Cartouches." In *The Truth in Painting,* Translated by Geoffrey Bennington and Ian McLeod, 183–253. Chicago: University of Chicago Press, 1987.

– "Choreographies." In *The Ear of the Other,* 163–85.

– "Des Tours de Babel." Translated by Joseph F. Graham. In Joseph F. Graham, ed., *Difference in Translation,* 165–207. Ithaca: Cornell University Press, 1985.

– *The Ear of the Other: Otobiography, Transference, Translation.* Edited by Christie V. McDonald, translated by Peggy Kamuf. New York: Schocken, 1985.

– "Economimesis." Translated by R. Klein. *Diacritics* 11, no. 2 (Summer 1981): 3–25.

- "Envois." In *The Post Card*, 3–256.
- "*Fors*: The Anglish Words of Nicolas Abraham and Maria Torok." Translated by Barbara Johnson. In Abraham and Torok, *The Wolf Man's Magic Word*, xi–xlviii.
- "Freud and the Scene of Writing." In *Writing and Difference*, 196–231.
- *Glas*. Translated by John P. Leavy, Jr. and Richard Rand. Lincoln: University of Nebraska Press, 1990.
- "Living On – Border Lines." Translated by James Hulbert. In Peggy Kamuf, ed., *A Derrida Reader*, 256–68.
- *Memoires for Paul de Man*. Rev. ed. Translated by Cecile Lindsay, Jonathan Culler, Eduardo Cadava, and Peggy Kamuf. New York: Columbia University Press, 1986.
- "Mnemosyne." Translated by Cecile Lindsay. In *Memoires: For Paul de Man*, 1–43.
- "Notices (Warnings)." In *The Post Card*.
- *Of Grammatology*. Translated by Gayatri Chakravorty Spivak. Baltimore: Johns Hopkins University Press, 1976.
- "Otobiographies: The Teaching of Nietzsche and the Politics of the Proper Name." In *The Ear of the Other*, 1–38.
- "Passe-Partout." *The Truth in Painting*. Translated by Geoffrey Bennington and Ian McLeod, 1–14. Chicago: University of Chicago Press, 1987.
- "Plato's Pharmacy." In *Dissemination*. Translated by Barbara Johnson, 61–172. Chicago: University of Chicago Press, 1981.
- *Positions*. Translated by Alan Bass. Chicago: University of Chicago Press, 1981.
- *The Post Card: From Socrates to Freud and Beyond*. Translated by Alan Bass. Chicago: University of Chicago Press, 1987.
- "Psyche: Invention of the Other." In *Acts of Literature*, 310–43.
- "Roundtable on Autobiography." In *The Ear of the Other*, 39–90.
- "Roundtable on Translation." In *The Ear of the Other*, 91–162.
- "Shibboleth." Translated by Joshua Wilner. In *Acts of Literature*, 370–413.
- "Signature Event Context" In Kamuf, ed. *A Derrida Reader*, 80–111.
- *Specters of Marx: The State of the Debt, the Work of Mourning, and the New International*. Translated by Peggy Kamuf. New York: Routledge, 1994.
- *Speech and Phenomena and Other Essays on Husserl's Theory of Signs*. Translated by David B. Allison. Evanston: Northwestern University Press, 1973.
- "Structure, Sign, and Play in the Discourse of the Human Sciences." In *Writing and Difference*, 278–93.

- "The Theater of Cruelty." In *Writing and Difference*, 232–50.
- "'This Strange Institution Called Literature:' An Interview With Jacques Derrida." In *Acts of Literature*, 33–75.
- "To Speculate – On 'Freud.'" In *The Post Card*, 257–409.
- *Writing and Difference*. Translated by Alan Bass. Chicago: University of Chicago Press, 1978.

Doyle, Arthur Conan. "The Parasite." Website: www.literature.org/authors/doyle-arthur-conan/parasite/chapter-02.html

Fiedler, Leslie. *Love and Death in the American Novel*. Rev. ed. New York: Stein and Day, 1966.

Felman, Shoshana. *Jacques Lacan and the Adventure of Insight: Psychoanalysis in Contemporary Culture*. Cambridge, Mass.: Harvard University Press, 1987.

Forster, E.M. *Aspects of the Novel*. Hammondsworth: Penguin, 1976.

Foster, Dennis A. "J.G. Ballard's *Empire of the Senses*." *PMLA* 103, no. 3 (May, 1993): 519–32.

Foucault, Michel. "The Eye of Power: A Conversation with Jean-Pierre Barou and Michelle Perrot." Translated by Colin Gordon. In Colin Gordon, ed., *Power/Knowledge: Selected Interviews and Other Writings 1972–1977*, 146–65. New York: Pantheon, 1977.
- "Panopticism." In *Discipline and Punish*. Translated by Alan Sheridan, 195–230. New York: Vintage, 1977,

Freud, Sigmund. "The Case of the Wolf-Man." In *The Wolf-Man by the Wolf Man*. Edited by Muriel Gardiner, 153–262. New York: Basic Books, 1971.
- *The Interpretation of Dreams*. Vol. 4. London: Penguin,1976.
- "Mourning and Melancholia." *Standard Edition*. Vol. 14. 243–58.
- *The Standard Edition of the Complete Psychological Works of Sigmund Freud*. 24 vols. Translated by James Strachey. London: Hogarth, 1957.
- "The Uncanny." *Standard Edition*. Vol. 17. 219–56.

Gallop, Jane. *Reading Lacan*. Ithaca: Cornell University Press, 1985.

Gunn, Daniel. *Psychoanalysis and Fiction: An Exploration of Literary and Psychoanalytic Borders*. Cambridge, Mass.: Cambridge University Press, 1988.

Halberstam, Judith. *Skin Shows: Gothic Horror and the Technology of Monsters*. Durham: Duke University Press, 1995.

Haraway, Donna J. *Simians, Cyborgs, and Women: The Reinvention of Nature*. New York: Routledge, 1991.

Hartman, Geoffrey. *Saving the Text: Literature/Derrida/Philosophy*. Baltimore: Johns Hopkins University Press, 1981.

Hawthorne, Nathaniel. *The House of the Seven Gables*. New York: Bantam, 1981.

Heidegger, Martin. *An Introduction to Metaphysics*. Translated by Ralph Manheim. New Haven: Yale University Press, 1959.

– *Kant and the Problem of Metaphysics*. Translated by Richard Taft. Bloomington: Indiana University Press, 1990.

– "Letter on Humanism." *Basic Writings*. Edited by David Farrell Krell, 193–242. San Francisco: Harper Collins, 1977.

– "Poetically Man Dwells." In *Poetry, Language, Thought*, 213–29.

– "The Thing." *Poetry, Language, Thought*, 163–86.

– *Poetry, Language, Thought*. Translated by Albert Hofstadter. New York: Harper and Row, 1971.

Jameson, Fredric. *Postmodernism or, The Cultural Logic of Late Capitalism*. Durham: Duke University Press, 1992.

Jones, Alexander, ed. *The Jerusalem Bible: Reader's Edition*. Garden City, N.Y.: Doubleday,1966.

Kamuf, Peggy, ed. *A Derrida Reader: Between the Blinds*. New York: Columbia University Press, 1991

King, Stephen. *Danse Macabre*. New York: Berkley Books, 1983.

– *Pet Sematary*. Garden City, N.Y.: Doubleday, 1983.

Kristeva, Julia. "Holbein's Dead Christ." Translated by Leon S. Roudiez. In Michael Fehr, ed., *Zone: Fragments for a History of the Human Body–Part One*, 241–65. New York: Urzone Inc., n.d.

– "Revolution in Poetic Language." Translated by Margaret Waller. In Toril Moi, ed., *The Kristeva Reader*, 90–136. New York: Columbia University Press, 1986.

– *Powers of Horror: An Essay on Abjection*. Translated by Leon S. Roudiez. New York: Columbia University Press, 1982.

– *Desire in Language: A Semiotic Approach to Literature and Art*. Translated by Thomas Gora, Alice Jardine, and Leon S. Roudiez. New York: Columbia University Press, 1980.

Lacan, Jacques. "Agency of the Letter in the Unconscious." In *Écrits*. Translated by Alan Sheridan, 146–78. New York and London: W.W. Norton and Company, 1977.

– "The Mirror Stage as Formative of the Function of the I as Revealed in Psychoanalytic Experience." In *Écrits*, 1–7.

Le Fanu, J. Sheridan. "Carmilla." 1872; *The Penguin Book of Vampire Stories*. Alan Ryan, ed., 71–138. New York: Penguin, 1987.

Lessing, Doris. *Prisons We Choose to Live Inside*. Montreal: CBC Enterprises, 1986.

Massé, Michelle A. "Gothic Repetition: Husbands, Horrors, and Things That Go Bump In the Night." *Signs* 15, no. 4 (Summer 1990): 679–709.

McDonald, Christie. Preface to *The Ear of the Other*, by Jacques Derrida, vii–x.

Moorjani, Angela. *The Aesthetics of Loss and Lessness*. London: Macmillan, 1992.

Nussey, Kent. "Filling in the Millennium." *Brick* 53 (Winter 1996): 22–5.

Parker-Gounelas, Ruth. "Anachrony and Atopia: Specters of Marx, Derrida and Gothic Fiction." In *Ghosts: Deconstruction, Psychoanalysis, History*. New York: St. Martin's Press, 1999.

Pharr, Mary Ferguson. "A Dream of New Life: Stephen King's *Pet Sematary* as a Variant of *Frankenstein*." In *The Gothic World of Stephen King: Landscape of Nightmares*. Gary Hoppenstand and Ray B. Browne, eds. Bowling Green, Ohio: Bowling Green State University Press, 1987.

Poe, Edgar Allan. "The Fall of the House of Usher." *The Unabridged Edgar Allan Poe*. Philadelphia: Running Press, 1983.

Polidori, John. "The Vampyre." *The Vampyre and Other Works: Selected Writings of Dr. John Polidori*, 5–23. Kent: Gargoyle's Head Press, 1991.

Rand, Nicholas T. Introduction and various editor's notes to *The Shell and the Kernel*, by Abraham and Torok.

– Translator's Introduction to *The Wolf Man's Magis Word: A Cryptonomy*, by Abraham and Torok, li–lxix.

Rashkin, Esther. *Family Secrets and the Psychoanalysis of Narrative*. Princeton: Princeton University Press, 1992.

Rice, Anne. *Interview with the Vampire*. New York: Alfred A. Knopf, 1976.

– *The Vampire Lestat: Book Two of the Vampire Chronicles*. New York: Ballantine, 1995.

Riddel, Joseph N. *Purloined Letters: Originality and Repetition in American Literature*. Edited by Mark Bauerlein. Baton Rouge: Louisiana State University Press, 1995.

Royle, Nicholas. *Telepathy and Literature: Essays on the Reading Mind*. Cambridge, Mass.: Basil Blackwell, 1991.

Schehr, Lawrence. "Djuna Barnes' *Nightwood*: Dismantling the Folds." *Style* 19, no. 1, (Spring 1985):36–49.

Schor, Esther. *Bearing the Dead: The British Culture of Mourning From the Enlightenment to Victoria*. Princeton: Princeton University Press, 1994.

Sedgwick, Eve Kosofsky. *The Coherence of Gothic Conventions*. New York: Methuen, 1986.

Spivak, Gayatri Chakravorty. Translator's Preface to *Of Grammatology*, by Jacques Derrida, ix–lxxxvii.

Stirner, Max. *The Ego and Its Own*. Edited by David Leopold. Cambridge, Mass.: Cambridge University Press, 1995.

Stoker, Bram. *Dracula*. New York: Oxford University Press, 1983.

Summers, Montague. *The Vampire in Europe*. New Hyde Park, N.Y.: University Books, 1962.

Taylor, Mark C. *Nots*. Chicago: University of Chicago Press, 1983.

Torok, Maria. "Fantasy: An Attempt to Define Its Structure and Operation." In Abraham and Torok, *The Shell and the Kernel*, 27–36.

– "The Illness of Mourning and the Fantasy of the Exquisite Corpse." In Abraham and Torok, *The Shell and the Kernel*, 107–24.

– "Story of Fear: The Symptoms of Phobia – the Return of the Repressed or the Return of the Phantom?" In Abraham and Torok, *The Shell and the Kernel*, 177–86.

Tropp, Martin. *Images of Fear: How Horror Stories Helped Shape Modern Culture (1818–1918)*. Jefferson, N.C.: McFarland, 1990.

Ulmer, Gregory. *Applied Grammatology: Post(e) Pedagogy from Jacques Derrida to Joseph Beuys*. Baltimore: Johns Hopkins University Press, 1985.

– "The Object of Post-Criticism." In *The Anti-Aesthetic: Essays on Postmodern Culture*. Ed. Hal Foster. Seattle: Bay, 1983.

– "Sounding the Unconscious." *Glassary*. by John P. Leavy, Jr. Lincoln: University of Nebraska Press, 1980.

Underwood, Tim, and Chuck Miller, eds. *Bare Bones: Conversations on Terror with Stephen King*. New York: Warner, 1988.

Wallace, Richard. "Malice in Wonderland." Excerpt from *Jack the Ripper: "Light-Hearted Friend."* Melrose, Mass.: Gemini Press. *Harper's Magazine* (November 1996): 37–39.

Waller, Gregory A. *The Living and the Undead: From Stoker's Dracula to Romero's Dawn of the Dead*. Urbana: University of Illinois Press, 1986.

Weir, Lorraine. *Writing Joyce: A Semiotics of the Joyce System*. Bloomington: Indiana University Press, 1989.

White, Hayden. *Metahistory: The Historical Imagination in Nineteenth-Century Europe*. Baltimore: Johns Hopkins University Press, 1973.

Wigley, Mark. *The Architecture of Deconstruction: Derrida's Haunt*. Cambridge, Mass.: MIT Press, 1993.

Williams, Anne. *Art of Darkness: A Poetics of Gothic*. Chicago: University of Chicago Press, 1995.

Yeats, William Butler. "The Second Coming." *The Poems of W.B. Yeats: A New Edition*. Edited by Richard J. Finneran. New York: MacMillan, 1924.

Žižek, Slavoj. *Looking Awry: An Introduction to Jacques Lacan through Popular Culture*. Cambridge, Mass.: MIT Press, 1993.

Index